A PHOT
SEA
OF SO

DOUW & ELISE STEYN

Struik Publishers
(A division of New Holland Publishing (South Africa) (Pty) Ltd)
Cornelis Struik House
80 McKenzie Street
Cape Town 8001

New Holland Publishing is a member of the Johnnic Publishing Group.
www.struik.co.za
Log on to our photographic website
www.imagesofafrica.co.za for an African experience.

First published 2002
10 9 8 7 6 5 4 3 2 1

Copyright © in text: Douw & Elise Steyn 2002
Copyright © in photographs: Douw & Elise Steyn 2002
Copyright © in line drawings: Douw Steyn 2002
Copyright © in maps: Douw & Elise Steyn 2002
Copyright © in published edition: Struik Publishers 2002

Publishing manager: Pippa Parker
Managing editor: Helen de Villiers
Editor: Katharina von Gerhardt
Designers: Dominic Robson, Bridgitte Chemaly
Cartographer: Robin Cox

Reproduction by Hirt and Carter Cape (Pty) Ltd
Printed and bound in Malaysia by Times Offset (M) Sdn Bhd

All rights reserved. No part of this publication may be reproduced, stored in a retrieval system, or transmitted, in any form or by any means, electronic, mechanical, photocopying, recording or otherwise, without the prior written permission of the copyright owners and publishers.

ISBN 1 86872 715 7

Imprint page: *Gyroscala lamellosa* (*see* p. 59)
Contents page: *Lambis lambis* (*see* p. 31)
Back page: *Spirula spirula* (*see* p. 115)

CONTENTS

Introduction	4
What is a shell?	4
Glossary	5
Habitat	7
Collecting shells	9
How to build a shell collection	10
How to use this book	11
Description of shells	12
Further reading	142
Scientific index	142

INTRODUCTION

In 1848 Dr. Ferdinand Krauss published *Südafrikanische Mollusken*, the first book devoted solely to South African sea shells. Since then numerous articles have appeared in journals and many books have been published. However, these books, with a few exceptions, are now out of print. The purpose of this guide is to provide the reader with a concise reference work to the many sea shells found along the southern African shores, by presenting detailed descriptions and other useful information on the shells most often encountered. A few uncommon and rare shells are also illustrated.

WHAT IS A SHELL?

Shells that wash up on the shore once belonged to small animals known as molluscs. A mollusc is a soft-bodied animal that is unsegmented, although the body can be divided into four basic parts: foot, head, mantle, and the viscera or internal organs.

The foot is a muscular structure that enables the mollusc to cling, crawl, burrow in sand, or even swim. The mantle secretes the shell, which functions as an external skeleton that supports and protects the soft body with its organs. A shell is composed mainly of calcium carbonate and a protein matrix of conchiolin, secreted by cells that line the edge of the mantle. Calcium is deposited in layers to thicken the shell during growth. A form of calcium known as aragonite reflects light, producing the shiny, mother-of-pearl lustre on the inner surface of, for example, abalones and pearl oysters. The sculpture, or decoration, of a shell results from folds and fringes on the mantle, forming a variety of unique scales, ridges, spines and tubercles. The colour and patterns are created by the intermittent secretion of pigments from metabolic waste derived from the diet of the animal. These pigments are mixed in with the calcium while it is still soft.

Not all molluscs have an outer skeleton in the form of a shell: the cephalopods (octopuses, squid and cuttlefish) have an internal structure, the cuttlebone, which is used for buoyancy regulation. The bottom-dwelling nudibranchs (sea slugs) have no external skeletal structure for protection – they defend themselves by secreting toxic chemicals. Their vivid colour patterns, which can be most attractive, warn predators of their unpleasant taste and toxicity.

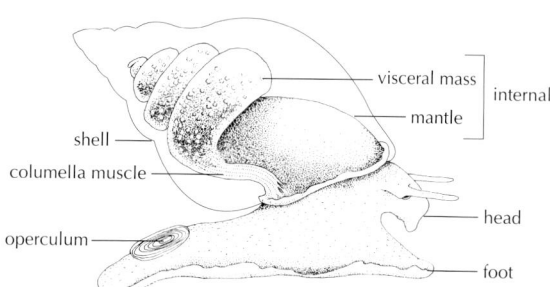

Internal structure of a mollusc

> ## Mollusc Classification
> **Phylum Mollusca:**
> Class Polyplacophora – chitons
> Class Cephalopoda – squid, octopuses, cuttlefish
> Class Bivalvia – mussels, clams, oysters
> Class Scaphopoda – tusk shells
> Class Gastropoda – snails
>   Subclass Prosobranchia – winkles, whelks, limpets
>   Subclass Opistobranchia – nudibranchs, sea slugs
>   Subclass Pulmonata – snails, slugs and false limpets

GLOSSARY

Anal canal: A notch at posterior end of aperture.
Annular ring: A circular ring on cowries.
Aperture: The opening of the shell through which the animal emerges.
Apex: The tip of the spire in a gastropod shell.
Articulated: Hinged together, as in the valves of bivalves.
Ascidian: Sea squirts, eg. redbait.
Basal spout: Spout-like extension of the outer lip near base of shell.
Bryozoan: Moss or lace animals.
Byssal sinus: Opening through which the byssus passes.
Byssus: Hairs or fibres, produced by a gland in the foot of many bivalves, which anchor bivalves to the substrate.
Callus pad: Thick deposit of calcium on or at the columella.
Cancellate: Sculpture formed by lines intersecting roughly at right angles.
Columella: Central column around which the gastropod shell is formed.
Coronations: Prominent nodules, often in a row.
Crenulate: With fine and regular notches or scallops.
Deposit feeder: An animal that uses a siphon to draw in food particles from the water.
Dorsum: Upper side of shell, opposite to aperture.
Denticle: A small tooth.
Ears: Extensions of the valves, near umbones, of pectens.
Encrusting organisms: Organisms that grow on the shell surface.
Endemic: Restricted to a particular area.
False umbilicus: An opening next to the true umbilicus.
Filter feeder: An animal that filters food particles from the water.
Form (fm.): Of the same species but with constant differences.
Fusiform: Spindle-shaped.
Granule: A fine grain-like bead.
Growth line: Fine axial or concentric line indicating previous position of the growing margin or edge.
Home-scar: Denuded area on rocks to which limpets return after grazing.
Hydroid: Feather-like sea fir.
Infratidal zone: An area below the tidal zone.
Intergrading: Breeding between two forms of the same species.
Interstices: Spaces between ribs or ridges.
Intertidal zone: Area between the high-tide and low-tide levels on the shore.
Jugal tract: (In chitons) The area on the mid-line of a valve where the sculpture differs from that of the adjacent area.
Labrum: Outer lip.
Lamellae: Thin, flattened blade-like protrusions.

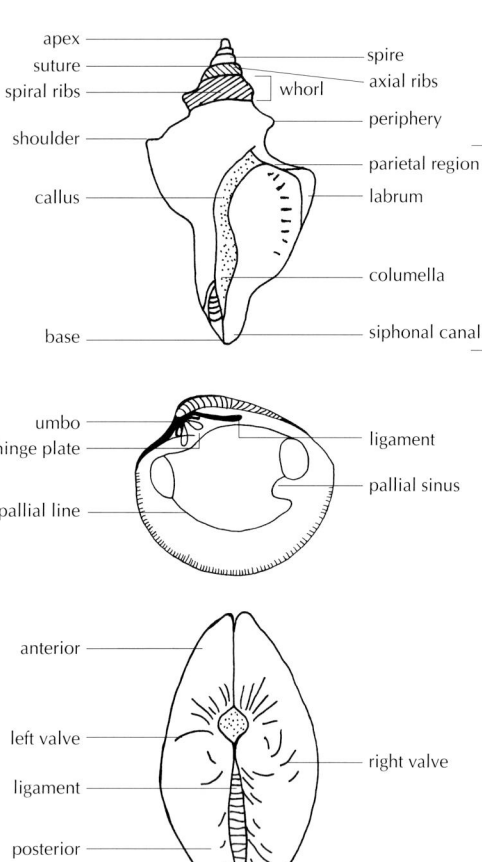

Different parts of a gastropod (top) and bivalve (middle and bottom)

Lira (pl. lirae): Small ridge.
Mantle-line: A line on the side of cowries where the two halves of the mantle meet when fully extended.
Mid-tidal: The area in the middle of the intertidal zone.
Muscle scar: An area for the attachment of a muscle.
Nacreous: Pearly.
Nodule: Small knob.
Operculum: Lid or cover used by gastropods to seal the aperture.
Orbicular: Ear-shaped.
Parietal: Part of the inner lip behind the columella or central pillar.
Parietal callus: Callus behind the columella.
Pelagic: Floating or free-swimming.

Periostracum: Superficial layer of fibrous material that covers, protects and camouflages the shell.
Periphery: Outermost point of a whorl where it bulges most.
Plica (pl. plicae): Fold.
Plicate: With folds.
Polychaete: Bristle-worm.
Protoconch: Embryonic or very early stage of the shell of a gastropod.
Pustule: A small tubercle.
Pyriform: Pear-shaped.
Pyura: Redbait.
Radial ribs: Ribs running from the central part of the shell to the margin.
Radial threads: Small ridges running from central part of shell to margin.
Radula: Ribbon-like tongue with minute teeth in a mollusc.
Riblets: Small ribs.
Sculpture: Ornamentation of the exterior of the shell.
Septum: Partition.
Shoulder: Prominent part of the whorl.
Siphon: A tube through which water enters or leaves the body.
Siphonal canal: Canal situated at anterior end of aperture.
Spicule: Minute spines.
Spindles: Bundles of spines.
Spiral keel: A prominent angular ridge or border.
Spire: Part of shell that includes all the whorls except the body whorl.
Stria (pl. striae): A fine line.
Stromboid notch: A notch near the anterior end of the outer lip in members of the Strombidae.
Sulcus: A groove.
Suture: The spiral groove at the junction of adjacent whorls.
Thread: A fine ridge.
Tubercle: Knob.
Tunicate: Sea squirt. The adult is a sessile filter-feeder.
Umbilicus: A circular opening usually in the base of the columella.
Umbo (pl. umbones): The dorsal peak on the valve of a bivalve shell.
Umbonal refection: A ridge running from umbo to margin of the shell.
Varix (pl. varices): Axial rib formed on gastropod shell during a previous rest period.
Veliger: An early stage in the development of a mollusc.
Whorl: One complete revolution of a gastropod shell.
Zooplankton: Planktonic animals.

HABITAT

Two major currents sweep along the southern African coast. The warm Agulhas current flows down the East coast and brings with it a plethora of Indo-Pacific species, which add to the immense diversity of molluscs found here. To the west, the colder Benguela current flows northwards. Wind-driven upwelling events bring cold nutrient-rich water from the depths to the surface. Species diversity is less marked than on the East coast, but abundance of marine species is higher.

A high percentage of temperate endemic molluscs occur along the Cape South coast where water temperatures are not as low as on the West coast but lower than on the East coast. Shells like *Cypraea edentula*, *Cypraea capensis* and *Trivia aperta* are endemic to this region.

Southern Africa's major ocean currents

Molluscs have adapted to a wide variety of physical factors such as light intensity, temperature, wave action and salinity levels. All these factors vary from one habitat to another, and influence the growth, shape, diet, breeding habits, colour and tenacity of the animals. The area above the high water mark, the splash zone, is marked by a relative absence of species, as factors such as dessication by sun and wind, and low nutrient availability come into play. Small periwinkles (Littorinidae) are able to live here as they have physically adapted to minimize dessication.

The littoral region or intertidal zone that lies between the high and low water mark supports a rich variety of molluscs such as limpets, mussels, oysters, trochids and nerites. These molluscs have evolved different ways of fixing themselves to the substrate so as not to get swept off the rocks by heavy wave action: limpets have a large foot with which they fasten themselves to the rock. Their flat, cone-shaped shell furthermore reduces the effect of the pounding waves by minimizing the drag of the receding waves. Mussels attach themselves to the rocks with strong byssus threads, while oysters secrete a calcerous cement. Flattened chitons too can be found on exposed rocks as they rely on the adhesive strength of their muscular foot to anchor them against the force of the waves. A robust shell, as in the topshells, also resists and minimizes wave damage.

Rock pools and rock crevices provide shelter for trochids, false limpets and limpets, while sandy shores are home to a variety of burrowing bivalves such as white mussels and ploughshare shells. In estuaries, mud and sand are mixed to provide a food-rich habitat for many molluscs such as pencil-bait and cockles.

Coral reefs and particularly the coral rubble harbour a variety of spectacular molluscan species. The tropical and sunny region with its warmer water creates conditions most congenial for molluscs, as food is prolific and growth is rapid.

Pelagic molluscs live near the ocean surface, where there is an abundance of sunlight and planktonic food. Some molluscs float by forming bubble rafts, while others attach themselves to floating objects such as seaweed.

Even the abyssal depths of the ocean are not free of molluscs. At this depth there is no light, and molluscs with shells usually lack colour. Cephalopods (like squid) generate phosphorescent blue, white and red lights in order to communicate with each other.

It is crucial that marine habitats are preserved. Shell collectors should treat these areas with respect and not overturn rocks or coral slabs without putting them back into their original position. Shell collectors should play an active part in the prevention of pollution, which is probably the main cause of the deterioration of marine life on our shores.

COLLECTING SHELLS

Beach combing is the easiest way to collect empty shells. Some beaches, for example Jeffreys Bay, are well known for the abundance and variety of shells that wash up there, particularly after storms. It is easier to collect shells on the beach during neap tides when the water is calmer than at spring tide, when the water is rough and few shells remain on the beach. However, beached shells are frequently worn and of poor quality. The intertidal zone may provide collectors with a more rewarding hunting ground.

Loose rocks in intertidal and tidal swimming pools can be overturned to look for live molluscs. Crevices and overhanging ledges should also be inspected for the more elusive mollusc.

Some molluscs such as limpets and chitons cling to rocks with such force that it is impossible to remove them by hand. A knife or spatula should be slid under the shell in order to dislodge it from the rock.

Burrowing gastropods leave trails in pools with sandy bottoms. A small sand mound is visible at the end of the trail; this reveals where the gastropod lies hidden. A siphon protruding above the sand surface indicates the presence of bivalves. Beds of eelgrass should also be investigated as many gastropods, particularly the smaller ones, find shelter here. A mangrove swamp is another home to a variety of molluscs, which cling to the roots and stems of trees, while others burrow in mud.

Molluscs are mainly cryptic animals that hide during the day. Collecting at night can be very productive as animals come out to feed. It is unwise to collect alone as incoming tides and heavy wave action pose serious threats. Always go in a group, suitably equipped with proper lights and protective, non-skid shoes.

Shells from deeper waters do not wash up on the beach. They can be obtained from divers, and from boats that dredge or trawl. Exchanging shells with other collectors can prove to be most satisfying. Buying shells from dealers or other collectors can also be rewarding although it is usually expensive.

Collectors are reminded that a permit is required to collect live molluscs, and when

Chiton tulipa.
A chiton may be difficult to dislodge

diving for shells using SCUBA equipment. The techniques and equipment required for snorkelling, scuba diving, trawling and dredging can be found in appropriate publications. Relevant permits can be obtained from post offices in the coastal regions. Collectors must refrain from taking more specimens than needed; we must preserve rather than decimate our natural heritage.

HOW TO BUILD A SHELL COLLECTION

Molluscs consist of some 100 000 species – the potential scope of a shell collection is thus vast and rather overwhelming. In this book the focus is on marine molluscs, although many collectors include land snails in their collection. At the outset, it is imperative to define the limits of the collection – decide whether to restrict it to a few families on a world-wide basis, whether to collect shells that are exclusively South African or to restrict sampling to beached shells only. Remember too that gift shops and shell dealers can be approached for rare species.

It is important to record details regarding the collected shells. The locality, habitat, date, circumstances, name of the collector and tide particulars must be recorded at the time of collection as these details all contribute to the shells' individual histories. Do not rely on memory. Shell identification can take place at a later stage.

Empty and live shells need to be cleaned and scrubbed. Beach shells are usually fairly clean and may require a wash in clean water and a light brushing using a nailbrush. However, shells are frequently encrusted with marine growths such as seaweeds, tubeworms, barnacles and other calcium deposits, while the periostracum may obscure the true colours of the shell.

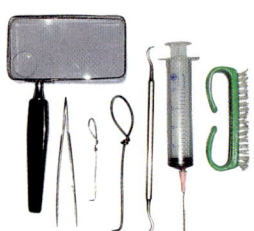

Shell cleaning instruments

The first step is to wash the shells in clean fresh water. Crabbed shells can become very unpleasant if the crab is not removed. To remove the animal from its shell, immerse the shell in water, slowly bring it to boil (5 minutes), and then allow it to cool slowly. The snail or crab can then be removed using forceps. Bivalves usually gape when immersed in boiling water or when left in fresh water. A strong jet of water directed into the shell should complete the cleansing process. Shells can be immersed in concentrated or diluted bleach for an hour or even overnight to help remove encrusting organisms and the periostracum. Remove any encrustations using crochet hooks, dental probes or homemade hooks and a stiff brush.

Note that glossy shells such as cowries should not be immersed in fresh water and should not be boiled. Small cracks develop on the surface due to the heat and the changing temperatures during freezing and thawing. To prevent damage, allow the mollusc to decay in moist sand before cleaning out the animal.

Beached shells may at times appear very dull. Such shells can be treated with technical oil using a soft cloth, which will bring out the colours and may even preserve the beauty of the shell for longer.

Once the shells are clean, they are ready to be stored. The shell, with the correct label, can be housed in a plastic box, match box, glass tube, clear polythene bag or any similar container lined with soft material, to prevent the shell from sliding around and getting scratched. Shells left exposed to light fade and lose their splendour and richness of colours. Rather store your collection in steel, plastic or wooden cabinets with flat drawers. Shells from the same family may vary considerably in size, so drawers should be interchangeable, and must make allowance for specimens of different size.

Shells are best displayed in trays

Identification is done at this stage. Compare your shell with the illustrations in books or consult fellow collectors. It is customary to enter the family, genus and species names as well as the describer of the shell and the date on which the shell was first described.

The reader is advised to do as much research as possible. Some of the older books that are out of print are still available in museums and libraries. A good idea is to join a shell club, consult the more experienced collectors and attend talks and exhibitions. Learning and understanding of molluscan diversity and biology can only increase and deepen the appreciation and respect of every collector.

HOW TO USE THIS BOOK

This book has been designed with the assumption that the reader will use it mainly as a field and photo guide. Two photographs per species account facilitate identification, as they present the front and back view of the shell. A distribution map of the southern African coast accompanies each species account. The average length of each shell is given in mm, and is measured from tip (apex) to base. A common or colloquial name is given for some shells only, as not all shells have common names. In some cases the common name refers to a group of shells collectively. The members of the Genus *Bullia*, for instance, are all known as ploughshare shells. Common names may also differ from region to region and the reader is strongly advised to master the scientific names. The occurrence of the shell is given as abundant, common, uncommon and rare. This refers to the occurrence of shells on the beach and in the intertidal zone. Shells that are rare on the beach may be abundant in deeper water.

Each species account is divided into five subsections: **Description** details the sculpture of the shell. **Colour** describes mostly the exterior colour, unless specified otherwise. **Habitat** indicates at what depths the live molluscs may be found. **Diet** refers to the live mollusc and what plants or animals it eats. **Notes** aid in differentiating between similar species, or highlight interesting information unique to a species.

Haliotis midae
Family Haliotidae (Abalones)

Common
160 mm

Description: This heavy shell is the largest of the family occurring in the region, reaching up to 200 mm. 8–11 perforations mark the exterior surface, which is sculptured by wavy corrugations running obliquely to growth-lines. Juveniles have fine spiral striae, and may be confused with *H. spadicea*. **Colour:** Purplish-brown to reddish-pink exterior. Interior is lined with mother-of-pearl. **Habitat:** Below low tide level, down to 25 m. **Diet:** Large seaweeds. **Notes:** Over-exploitation due to export is a real danger, as species only reaches sexual maturity at 8–10 years.

Haliotis spadicea
Family Haliotidae (Abalones)

Common
70 mm

Description: An ear-shaped shell with a concave outer lip and a smooth exterior. Iridescent green dots are present on the growth-lines and on the spiral striae in juveniles. Five to eight perforations occur along the periphery. **Colour:** Reddish- to purplish-brown exterior, speckled with white. Glossy interior has an orange-red stain below the spire. **Habitat:** Under rocks, along upper fringes of the intertidal zone among redbait. **Diet:** Grazes on algae. **Notes:** The 'Venus Ear' is used extensively by fisherman as bait, and is also known as 'Siffie'.

Haliotis parva
Family Haliotidae (Abalones)

Uncommon
45 mm

Description: This shell is ear-shaped like *Haliotis spadicea*, but smaller and lighter. A conspicuous spiral ridge runs along its mid-line parallel to the outer edge. A second ridge bears six to seven perforations on low nodules. Sculpture of fine spiral striae. **Colour:** Exterior ranges from purplish to reddish brown, orange or mottled with white, red or green. Interior is glossy. **Habitat:** Mostly infratidal. Empty shells are washed up on the beach. **Diet:** Grazes on algae. **Notes:** Animals are consumed by several reef fishes.

Dendrofissurella scutellum
Family Fissurellidae (Keyhole Limpets)

Common
35 mm

Description: Both ends of this thick shell are raised, it therefore never lies flat on an even surface. The exterior is covered with fine radial threads. The outer margin is slightly thickened while the inner margin is smooth or weakly crenulate. **Colour:** Exterior varies from dark brown to pink and grey, with dark radiating streaks. Interior is white. **Habitat:** Low-tide pools. **Diet:** Grazes on algae. **Notes:** Two subspecies occur, their ranges meeting at False Bay: *D. s. scutellum* is found to the west and is replaced by *D. s. hiantula* to the east.

Diodora calyculata — Common
Family Fissurellidae (Keyhole Limpets) — 28 mm

Description: This shell has a small and circular aperture. Faint and prominent radial ribs cover the exterior surface. Four strong radial ribs occur posteriorly. Weaker concentric striae form small nodules where they cross the radial ribs. **Colour:** Greyish brown or pinkish brown with dark brown radiating streaks. **Habitat:** Infratidal. Beach shells are common. **Diet:** Grazes on algae. **Notes:** The shell and apex are more elevated than in other members of this genus.

Diodora elizabethae — Common
Family Fissurellidae (Keyhole Limpets) — 35 mm

Description: A depressed shell with a small and rounded aperture. Nine strong radial ribs project from the outer margin. Four posterior ribs are particularly prominent. Concentric ridges form large flattened nodules where they cross the main ribs. **Colour:** Buff grey to light brown. Main ribs are tinged with pink. **Habitat:** Infratidal. Empty shells are common on the beach. **Diet:** Herbivorous, little known about the diet. **Notes:** These limpets are popularly used in shell craft in Jeffreys Bay where they are known as 'Duck Feet'.

Pupillaea aperta
Family Fissurellidae (Keyhole Limpets)

Common
35 mm

Description: A solid, oblong shell with a large oval hole occupying the central part of the shell. The white inner margin projects about 1 mm beyond the colourful outer layer. The radial threads are crossed by growth-lines. **Colour:** Grey, fawn or buff-pink with dark grey or brown rays radiating from the aperture. **Habitat:** Low-tide levels in crevices under rocks. **Diet:** Herbivorous, most probably feeds on algae. **Notes:** The animal appears slug-like as the shell is almost completely covered by the mantle.

Cymbula miniata
Family Patellidae (Limpets)

Common
75 mm

Description: A thin, nearly oval and low-domed shell. Dense, prickly riblets cover the surface. The margin may be smooth or crenulate. **Colour:** Radiating pink or red rays mark the pale exterior. The interior is milky with a bluish sheen over the pink rays. **Habitat:** Low-tide pools down to 10 m. **Diet:** Scrapes algae off the rock surface, forming an ill-defined home-scar. **Notes:** Two sub-species occur: *C. m. miniata* ranges from Namibia to the western Transkei and the more robust *C. m. sanguinans* with its broader, darker streaks replaces it in KwaZulu-Natal.

Cymbula compressa
Family Patellidae (Limpets)

Common
95 mm

Description: A light, compressed and high-domed shell with an oblong aperture. The surface is sculptured by slender radial riblets of differing sizes. **Colour:** Exterior is dull brown, paling towards the apex. Interior is pearly grey, turning brown towards the outer edge. **Habitat:** Adapted to live on the giant kelp *Ecklonia maxima*. **Diet:** Fronts and stems of the kelp. **Notes:** Juveniles cling to the fronts of the kelp and move down the stems with age, where the adults form scars on the stems. One of the first southern African shells described (Linnaeus, 1758).

Cymbula oculus
Family Patellidae (Limpets)

Common
90 mm

Description: A flat and broadly oval shell. The eroded exterior is distinguished by ten radiating ridges, which project from the margin. **Colour:** Dull greenish-brown to black exterior, while the interior is black or dark brown with a bluish border circling the light brown to cream muscle scar. **Habitat:** Lower intertidal zone. **Diet:** Grazes on algae. **Notes:** The animal begins its life as a male but changes into a female between two and three years of age.

Cymbula granatina
Family Patellidae (Limpets)

Common
75 mm

Description: An oval, fairly low-domed shell with seven strong, angular ribs forming lateral projections. The shell surface is marked with concentric zigzag patterning, which is more prominent in juveniles. **Colour:** Juveniles are flecked green. The interior of adult shells is a shiny dark brown with a bluish border around the muscle scar, sometimes mottled with brown. Exterior is greyish brown. **Habitat:** Clings to mid-tidal rocks, forms a home-scar. **Diet:** Scrapes algae off rocks. **Notes:** High densities of tall domed shells occur in Namaqualand.

Scutellastra argenvillei
Family Patellidae (Limpets)

Common
90 mm

Description: A tall, oval shell with a high dome. The surface is finely ridged with flattened riblets that project slightly at the margin, forming distinct 'teeth'. The exterior is always eroded and encrusted. **Colour:** The exterior is dark brown to black while the interior is porcelain-white with a pale orange or brown centre. **Habitat:** Exposed rocks at the low-water spring-tide level, forming home-scars. **Diet:** Feeds on algae. **Notes:** Juveniles inhabit the dorsum of adult shells.

Scutellastra longicosta
Family Patellidae (Limpets)

Common
60 mm

Description: A depressed shell with 7–11 large projecting ribs that render it star-shaped, which is particularly evident in juveniles. The outline is normally more rounded in adults. **Colour:** Exterior is almost black, and mostly eroded. Interior is bluish white with a brownish centre and a black marginal band. **Habitat:** Lower mid-tidal region on home-scars. **Diet:** *Ralfsia* algae, which surround the home-scar. **Notes:** Specimens from KwaZulu-Natal have no projecting ribs.

Scutellastra cochlear
Family Patellidae (Limpets)

Common
65 mm

Description: A distinctively pear-shaped shell, often encrusted by coralline algae and other marine growth. Juveniles live on the shells of adults where they form home-scars. Broad, flat and unequal ribs occur on the shell, which project minimally at the margin. **Colour:** White exterior has beige rays, while the white interior is tinged blue, and has a raised black muscle scar. **Habitat:** Infratidal fringe in a narrow, densely populated belt. **Diet:** Feeds on algae. **Notes:** The belt occupied by these animals is referred to as the 'Cochlear zone'.

Scutellastra tabularis
Family Patellidae (Limpets)

Common
100 mm

Description: This is the largest southern African limpet. It is fairly flat, heavy and oval. 30 fairly flat, equally sized ribs project slightly at the margin. The ribs are scaly in juveniles. **Colour:** Exterior is brownish red and the interior is white with a dark pink or red irregular rim. **Habitat:** On rocks at the infratidal fringe and down to about 4 m. **Diet:** Feeds on *Ralfsia* algae. **Notes:** The animals form distinct home-scars, which they leave only in order to feed.

Helcion concolor
Family Patellidae (Limpets)

Common
40 mm

Description: A delicate shell that is depressed and egg-shaped in outline. Sculpture of more or less equally prominent riblets. The margin is smooth. **Colour:** The exterior colour ranges from yellow, brown to black, with radiating brown streaks, rays or dots. The interior is similar to the exterior but has a light brown or orange centre. **Habitat:** Mainly in the mid-tidal region. **Diet:** Grazes on small encrusting plants and animals. **Notes:** The animals form distinct home-scars.

Calliostoma ornatum
Family Trochidae (Top Shells)

Common
20 mm

Description: This shell has the outline of an equilateral triangle. The sides of the spire are slightly concave and the sutures are shallow. The periphery of the body whorl is angular. Fine granular ridges with two to three prominent ridges occur on the lower part of each whorl. **Colour:** Various shades of brown or violet with patches of darker brown on the periphery, while the inside of the aperture is shiny. **Habitat:** Low intertidal zone down to 50 m. **Diet:** Presumably feeds on sea fans. **Notes:** This is the most common of the *Calliostoma* species.

Clanculus puniceus
Family Trochidae (Top Shells)

Common
20 mm

Description: The shell width is greater than the shell height and the opening of the umbilicus is wide. Callus covers half the base area. Wavy ridges extend from the umbilicus over the callus. Strong teeth occur at the base of the columella. Spiral rows of granules occur on the whorls. **Colour:** Brick-red, with two rows of black dots on each whorl and on the base. White dots occur on some granules. **Habitat:** Usually lives infratidally. Rarely found in sheltered pools. **Diet:** Herbivorous. **Notes:** Sometimes referred to as a 'Strawberry' due to its colour.

Monodonta australis
Family Trochidae (Top Shells)

Common
35 mm

Description: A thick shell with rounded whorls. Spiral ridges are flattened and the umbilicus is closed by callus. The inner aperture is ridged, and the inner lip has a thick callus that forms a single sharp tooth projecting inward. **Colour:** Usually buff-green or pale brown. Rectangular brownish-black spots alternate with paler spots on ridges. Inner edge of outer lip is green. Inner lip bears a white callus. **Habitat:** Intertidal, lives in crevices on rocks and pools. **Diet:** Grazes on algae. **Notes:** Frequently found high up on intertidal rocks.

Diloma tigrina
Family Trochidae (Top Shells)

Abundant
35 mm

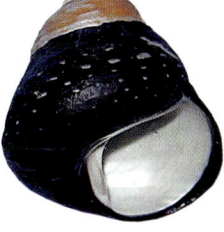

Description: A wide shell with a slightly raised spire that is usually eroded. The surface is sculptured by low spiral ridges that are conspicuous in juveniles but eroded in adults. The umbilicus is absent. **Colour:** Black, with scattered white dots on lower whorls. Inner aperture is iridescent. The inner edge of the outer lip has a black border. The columella is white. **Habitat:** Mid-tidal region where it lives on and under rocks. **Diet:** Grazes on algae. **Notes:** Sometimes harvested for food.

Diloma sinensis
Family Trochidae (Top Shells)

Common
40 mm

Description: The shell width is greater than the shell height. It has a blunt spire and rounded whorls with a strongly curved periphery. The flat base has a concave callus. The umbilicus is absent. Fine spiral sculpture marks the exterior in juveniles. The presence of growth-lines distinguishes the adults. **Colour:** Purplish black but the columella is white with a distinctive rose-coloured basal blotch. **Habitat:** Found on rocky shores at low spring-tide level. **Diet:** Grazes on algae. **Notes:** May be harvested for food.

Diloma variegata
Family Trochidae (Top Shells)

Abundant
20 mm

Description: The shell width is equal to the shell height. Spiral threads differentiate the juveniles from the adults. The umbilicus is covered by a white callus. The inner aperture is iridescent and the inner lip is grooved. **Colour:** Usually speckled or streaked with grey, orange, brown, green or yellow. A row of dark and light square flecks occur below the suture. The interior is shiny. **Habitat:** Intertidal rocky shores. Juveniles live lower on the shore than adults. **Diet:** Grazes on algae. **Notes:** Adults move up-shore away from predators such as starfish and whelks.

Diloma tabularis
Family Trochidae (Top Shells)

Abundant
15 mm

Description: This shell has a smooth surface, convex whorls and a fairly high spire. The umbilicus is covered with a white callus. The inner surface of the aperture is nacreous, and the outer lip is grooved inside. **Colour:** Zigzag reddish-brown bands separated by pale buff axial rays, bounded by green and red lines. **Habitat:** High neap-tide level where it clings to rocks; also in shallow pools. **Diet:** Mainly algae. **Notes:** This species almost completely replaces *Diloma variegata* in the warmer waters of KwaZulu-Natal.

Trochus nigropunctatus
Family Trochidae (Top Shells)

Common
26 mm

Description: The shell width is greater than the shell height. The spire is convex and the surface is covered with fine granular rows. Five spiral ridges occur on the base, and run into the inner aperture. The periphery of the body whorl is angular. The closed umbilicus is sunken, and is penetrated by three spiral cords. **Colour:** Buff-pink and green with dark axial blotches and streaks. **Habitat:** Cracks and crevices in mid-tidal rock pools, among seaweeds. **Diet:** Algae and seaweed. **Notes:** An active crawler that swivels its shell violently when attacked by a predator.

Turbo coronatus
Family Turbinidae (Turban Shells)

Common
45 mm

Description: The shell width is greater than the shell height. The apex is usually worn. The inner lip has a wide, concave callus. The exterior supports spiral rows of coarse nodules, some scale-like and pointed, others almost turreted. The granular operculum is tinged with green. **Colour:** Greyish green. Tips of nodules and edge of outer lip are green. **Habitat:** Mid-tidal region in pools, under rocks and in crevices. **Diet:** Small algae. **Notes:** The operculum (which looks like a round button) of dead animals frequently washes up on the beach.

Turbo sarmaticus
Family Turbinidae (Turban shells)

Common
100 mm

Description: This round turban shell is the largest of the family in southern Africa. The shoulder is covered with several rows of low and rounded nodules. Juveniles have ridges with strong nodules, which disappear in adults. The heavy operculum is densely packed with coarse knobs. **Colour:** Dull grey to dull olive. Underlying black layer prominent in some parts. Base of body whorl is orange. **Habitat:** Intertidal. **Diet:** Feeds on algae. **Notes:** The animal is used as bait and food, but harvest is regulated by law.

Turbo cidaris
Family Turbinidae (Turban Shells)

Common
38 mm

Description: The shell width is greater than the shell height. The smooth exterior may have weak spiral ridges and the whorls are rounded. The operculum is granular with a circular groove that spirals into a central pit. **Colour:** Large, cold-water shells are drab grey. Smaller specimens are reddish brown, speckled or streaked with green or orange. **Habitat:** Intertidal pools and crevices down to 10 m. **Diet:** Feeds on algae. **Notes:** The subspecies *T. c. natalensis* has strong spiral ridges, and the operculum is covered with blunt tubercles and has no spiral groove.

Turbo miliaris
Family Turbinidae (Turban Shells)

Uncommon
100 mm

Description: A large and fairly heavy shell with a prominent rounded body whorl. A concave area occurs below the suture, which is moderately deep. The fairly smooth exterior is marked by growth-lines and two rows of rounded nodules. The inner aperture is nacreous, with a narrow brown band at the inside edge of the outer lip. **Colour:** Brown with wavy flames. The spire is tinted with green. **Habitat:** Intertidal rocks and lower down. **Diet:** Herbivorous. **Notes:** The taxonomical status of this species is still uncertain; the species may be reclassified in the future.

Tricolia capensis
Family Phasianellidae (Pheasant Shells)

Abundant
20 mm

Description: A globular shell that is variable in shape and colour. The spire and aperture are equal in length and the smooth and glossy exterior bears faint striae. The calcareous operculum is white.
Colour: Brownish red, green or yellow, whereas beach shells are bright red with white, green or yellow; with wavy streaks or flames. **Habitat:** Lives among seaweed. **Diet:** Grazes on algae. **Notes:** Shells on the East coast are usually bigger and more globular than those from the West coast – they are generally known as 'Berries'.

Nerita albicilla
Family Neritidae (Nerites)

Common
25 mm

Description: A globular, depressed shell. The surface is marked by prominent, well spaced flat ribs. The columella bears distinct pustules and weak teeth and the outer lip has weakly developed teeth.
Colour: The granular operculum is grey. Ground colour is black with white blotches, sometimes black or with black spiral bands on a white background. **Habitat:** Large colonies in the upper mid-tidal region among rocks. **Diet:** Feeds on algae and lichen. **Notes:** Exterior frequently badly eroded.

Nerita textiles
Family Neritidae (Nerites)

Uncommon
35 mm

Description: One of the largest Nerites in the region. The exterior of the shell is rough with strong spiral ridges crossed by axial ribs. The columella bears nodules and the outer lip has a row of ridge-like teeth. The edge of the outer lip is crenulate. **Colour:** Dull white with black marks on ridges. Columella shield is bluish white or tinged with yellow. Granular operculum is bluish grey. **Habitat:** Upper intertidal zone in cracks and crevices on exposed rocks. **Diet:** Herbivorous. **Notes:** Highly valued by Pondo people as an ornament.

Nerita polita
Family Neritidae (Nerites)

Common
30 mm

Description: A heavy shell with a depressed spire. The smooth surface is glossy with wavy axial threads. The columella is smooth with two to three weak teeth and the operculum is covered by fine radiating threads. Peripheral area has fine ridges running perpendicular to the radiating threads. **Colour:** Grey, red, maroon or orange forming flecks or bands. Aperture is white, operculum is greyish yellow. **Habitat:** Buried in sand among rocks in the upper mid-tidal zone. **Diet:** Grazes on algae. **Notes:** Extremely attractive due to glossy surface and colour.

Nerita undata
Family Neritidae (Nerites)

Uncommon
35 mm

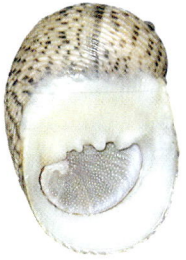

Description: A globular shell with a short spire and with numerous strong spiral cords with wide intervals on the surface. The columella shield bears weak, wavy folds. The inner lip has three to four strong denticles, while the outer lip carries a row of fine denticles; two are prominent posteriorly. **Colour:** Buff to yellow, cords marked with dark grey or black. Apex is yellow. Operculum is grey with pustules. **Habitat:** Roofs of caverns and overhanging rocks, in crevices at the high-water mark. **Diet:** Herbivorous. **Notes:** Larger older specimens are often badly eroded.

Nodilittorina knysnaensis
Family Littorinidae (Periwinkles)

Abundant
10 mm

Description: A squat shell with a fairly high spire and a rounded body whorl. The shell frequently has a thin spiral keel. The exterior is marked by fine spiral threads. **Colour:** Grey-brown to brownish black with paler bands below the suture and on the base, where it is flecked with yellow or white. Purplish-brown aperture is marked by a basal white band. **Habitat:** High up on the shore in crevices or on rock surfaces. **Diet:** Herbivorous. **Notes:** Hangs from rock surfaces by a mucus thread during the heat of the day.

Nodilittorina africana
Family Littorinidae (Periwinkles)

Abundant
10 mm

Description: This shell varies in shape. It is usually globular with a low spire, and with convex or rounded whorls. The periphery of the body whorl is rounded. The exterior is smooth and may have fine spiral threads. The aperture is rounded and the horny operculum is transparent. **Colour:** Blue to greyish white. Aperture is dark brown with a white edge. A white line extends into the aperture. **Habitat:** High up on the shore on exposed rocks. **Diet:** Grazes on algae. **Notes:** As *Nodilittorina* species occur in such abundance at the high-tide level, this area is also referred to as the Littorina zone.

Turitella carinifera
Family Turritellidae (Screw Shells)

Common
60 mm

Description: A shell with a broad base that tapers to a sharp point. The whorls are angular with one raised rib forming a keel. The basal margin is strongly angular. Fine spiral threads encircle all the whorls. Deformed specimens frequently occur. **Colour:** Creamy or dull grey to brown. Often flecked, and brown below the suture. **Habitat:** On sand under rocks in low tide pools and down to 100 m or more. **Diet:** Probably feeds on sponges and ascidians. **Notes:** Abundant and large in the Cape, but small in KwaZulu-Natal and Mozambique.

Strombus mutabilis
Family Strombidae (Conchs)

Common
30 mm

Description: This shell has a fairly high and sharp spire and a strong and rounded shoulder with low nodules. The exterior is sculptured by fine tubercles. Weak varices occur on the spire. The large body whorl is smooth. Fine spiral threads become more prominent with numerous weak ridges on the outer lip and on the columella. The outer lip is characteristically notched. **Colour:** Cream, yellow, speckled with spotted spiral lines. **Habitat:** In low-tide pools in crevices or in mud. **Diet:** Grazes on algae. **Notes:** Most common *Strombus* in southern Africa.

Strombus decorus
Family Strombidae (Conchs)

Rare
60 mm

Description: A conical shell with a low spire, covered with spiral and axial threads. The prominent rounded shoulder has a few faint folds. The aperture is narrow. The outer lip is marked by a posterior and stromboid notch. **Colour:** White with wavy dark brown axial lines or blotches arranged in spiral bands. Interior of aperture is orange. White edge occurs on the outer lip. **Habitat:** Infratidal. Shallow pools on sand and mud, or among rocks. **Diet:** Herbivorous. **Notes:** Rare in South Africa but fairly common in Mozambique.

Strombus gibberulus
Family Strombidae (Conchs)

Uncommon
68 mm

Description: A short-spired shell with prominent rounded varices and fine spiral threads. The spire and body whorl appear distorted. The shoulder is rounded. The exterior is smooth with spiral striae behind the lip and on the base. The columella is not very thick. **Colour:** White with many narrow brown lines. Columella and outer edge of lip are white. Interior of aperture is purple with white streaks. **Habitat:** Infratidal. In sand and mud in low-tide pools. **Diet:** Herbivorous. **Notes:** Uncommon, but may be found in tidal swimming pools.

Lambis lambis
Family Strombidae (Conchs)

Common
150 mm

Description: A solid shell with a short, wide anterior canal. The columella is fairly smooth. Small rounded nodules occur on the spire whorls. The heavy lip has seven digits, the most anterior digits are short. In females, the digits are longer and curved upwards. **Colour:** Uniform brown, decorated with vivid axial streaks of a deep reddish brown. **Habitat:** Lives mostly infratidally in shallow water. **Diet:** Herbivorous, grazes on seaweeds and algae. **Notes:** Also occurs in Fiji, Tonga and the Marshall Islands.

Lambis truncata
Family Strombidae (Conchs)

Uncommon
320 mm

Description: A solid shell with strong, large nodules on the spire whorls. The outer lip is thick and has seven or more digits. The aperture and columella are smooth and the stromboid notch is large and open. **Colour:** Off-white to beige, mottled with pinkish brown. Aperture is buff to light brown. **Habitat:** Inhabits shallow water, on sand and among rocks. **Diet:** Grazes on algae and seaweeds. **Notes:** This is one of the largest molluscs in the region.

Calyptraea chinensis
Family Calyptraeidae (Slipper Shells)

Common
20 mm

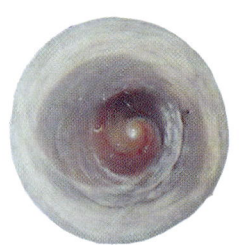 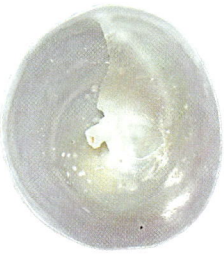

Description: The thin 'Chinese Hat' is circular in shape, and flat with a sharp central apex. The base is concave with an internal spiral partition that extends from apex to margin, forming a conspicuous lobe at its junction with the columella. The exterior is smooth with very fine spiral threads and a faint suture. The interior is glossy. **Colour:** Buff white, violet or brownish yellow. **Habitat:** Infratidal, down to 90 m. Empty shells frequently wash up on the shore. **Diet:** Filter feeder. **Notes:** Eastern shells are larger than those from the west.

Crepidula porcellana
Family Calyptraeidae (Slipper Shells)

Abundant
32 mm

Description: The shell shape varies with the substrate – some are flat, almost round; others are high and narrow. The exterior is smooth. The apex lies posteriorly, overhanging the shell margin, and the internal shelf is concave and notched. **Colour:** Dark to light brown, or mottled brown and white. The septum is white. **Habitat:** Infratidal. In rock pools; clinging to other shells. **Diet:** Filter feeder. **Notes:** Forms stacks with the smaller males at the top and the larger females at the bottom.

Natica allapapilionis
Family Naticidae (Moon Shells)

Uncommon
27 mm

Description: A globular shell with a raised spire. The body whorl is flattened below the deep suture. The umbilicus is entered by an oblique chord. The smooth, glossy exterior has radiating striae below the suture. **Colour:** Buff with four white lines evenly dotted with brown or red spots. Base is white. Operculum is white with curved radiating ridges. Brown periostracum. **Habitat:** Infratidal, burrowing in clean sand. **Diet:** Other molluscs. **Notes:** Despite the absence of eyes, a strong sense of smell enables the animal to detect prey from a distance.

Natica tecta
Family Naticidae (Moon Shells)

Common
30 mm

Description: The shell length is greater than the shell width. The spire is slightly raised and the globular body whorl with the umbilicus is completely covered by callus. The smooth exterior has fine growth-lines. **Colour:** Ground colour is yellow to yellowish brown, and flecked with dark brown. May have lighter lines with dark spots over body whorl, and subsutural oblique brown streaks. Columella callus is glossy white. **Habitat:** Infratidal, also in estuaries. **Diet:** Preys on gastropods and bivalves. **Notes:** Moon shells drill a hole through the shell of their prey by means of a radula – a tongue bearing ridge-like teeth.

Neverita peselephanti
Family Naticidae (Moon Shells)

Rare
50 mm

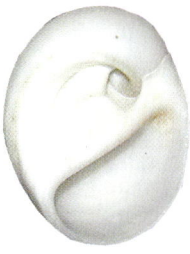

Description: The shell length is greater than the shell width. A large, heavy, globular shell with a fairly low spire. The aperture is moon-shaped and the glossy, fairly smooth exterior is marked with fine growth-lines. The base is slightly concave. The wide and curved umbilicus has a characteristic broad, flat ridge forming the margin of the umbilical opening. **Colour:** White, cream or light brown. Umbilicus and aperture are white inside. **Habitat:** Infratidal, in clean sand. **Diet:** Predator. **Notes:** Rare in South Africa but occurs in greater numbers further north.

Neverita didyma   Common
Family Naticidae (Moon Shells)   35 mm

Description: A globular shell, depressed with a low spire and a flattened base. The wide umbilicus is C-shaped and partly obscured by a callus pad. The callus pad is transected by a groove. A broad flattened ridge occurs on the edge of the umbilicus. The outer surface is smooth. **Colour:** Exterior is buff to bluish brown with a purplish apex, base crossed by irregular growth-lines. Umbilical callus dark brown and glossy, aperture is light brown. **Habitat:** Infratidal down to 50 m; common in beach-drift. **Diet:** Predator of molluscs. **Notes:** Known as 'Fish Eyes' in Jeffreys Bay.

Polinices mamilla   Common
Family Naticidae (Moon Shells)   45 mm

Description: The shell length is greater than the shell width. An oval, globular and smooth shell. The spire ranges from low to high. The umbilicus is obscured by a thick callus. **Colour:** Pure white, but may sometimes be stained, with a minute black spot on the apex of the protoconch. Periostracum is absent. Yellowish-brown operculum covers the entire aperture. **Habitat:** Burrows just below the surface in sand banks at low-tide level. **Diet:** Predator of gastropods and bivalves. **Notes:** The egg capsules form a tightly coiled egg-collar, typical for the genus *Polinices*.

Lamellaria nigra
Family Lamellariidae

Uncommon
35 mm

Description: A large, thin shell that is light and smooth. The spire is small and the early whorls are transparent. The aperture is very large. The exterior is sculptured by faint spiral striae and numerous coarse growth-lines on the later whorls. **Colour:** White, buff, tinged with light brown below the suture. **Habitat:** Infratidal, may be washed up on the beach with Pyura or redbait. **Diet:** Probably feeds on redbait. **Notes:** In the living animal, the mantle envelops the shell entirely, concealing it.

Trivia aperta
Family Triviidae (Trivias)

Common
20 mm

Description: A pyriform medium-sized shell with a wide aperture and a very narrow outer lip. The exterior is sculptured by coarse transverse ribs arising from denticles at the aperture. A medio-dorsal groove interrupts the transverse ridges. The spire is crossed by vertical riblets. **Colour:** Dorsum is pale pink, tinged with mauve. Base and ridges are white and not as glossy as the dorsum. **Habitat:** Infratidal. Beach shells are fairly common. **Diet:** Feeds on ascidians, the mantle matching the prey in colour. **Notes:** Known as 'Baby Toes' in Jeffreys Bay.

Trivia ovulata
Family Triviidae (Trivias)

Common
18 mm

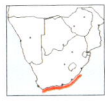

Description: Shell is smooth and has denticles on the inner edge of the outer lip. The exterior is sculptured by radial striae. The inner lip may have small teeth. Posterior and anterior extremities of the base are thicker than the median portion. The spire is elevated. **Colour:** Pure white to rose-pink or mauve-pink. Base and outer lip are white. **Habitat:** Lives in 8–10 m of water. Found on ascidians. **Diet:** Probably feeds on ascidians. **Notes:** Together with *T. aperta* they are called 'Baby Toes' in Jeffreys Bay.

Trivia magnidentata
Family Triviidae (Trivias)

Uncommon
20 mm

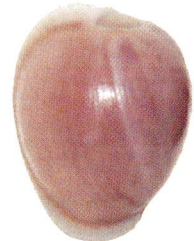

Description: A globular or pyriform shell, bulging within the posterior part. The spire is raised and not obscured by enamel and the aperture is wide. Coarse ribs extend over the outer lip. Prominent oblique ribs arise from the most anterior and posterior columellar denticles and continue over the shell base (a characteristic feature). **Colour:** Pink with a white base; cold-water specimens are paler. **Habitat:** Infratidal, on reefs at 20–50 m. **Diet:** Feeds on its tunicate host. **Notes:** The shell can be confused with *T. rubra*, which is an uncommon shell from the East coast.

Phenacovolva rosea
Family Ovulidae (False Cowries)

Rare
30 mm

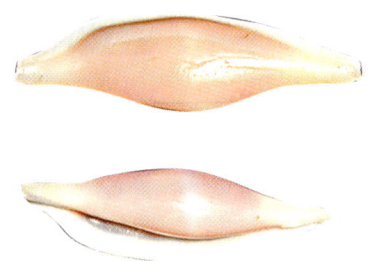

Description: A spindle-shaped shell. The exterior is smooth and glossy except for fine striae at both ends. The posterior extremity is longer than the anterior extremity. The aperture is long and much wider anteriorly than posteriorly. **Colour:** Pale pink and yellowish pink to red, sometimes with a light transverse median band. **Habitat:** Infratidal to a depth of 15 m or deeper. Empty shells wash up on the beach. **Diet:** Probably feeds on sea fans, to which it clings. **Notes:** Popular with shell collectors and known as 'Jam Tarts' in Jeffreys Bay.

Phenacovolva brevirostris
Family Ovulidae (False Cowries)

Rare
25 mm

Description: A spindle-shaped shell with relatively short extremities and a thick outer lip. The aperture is much wider at the anterior end. The extremities are sculptured by fine striae. The body whorl is usually smooth. **Colour:** Pink, orange to pinkish violet with a diffuse white median band. **Habitat:** Infratidal to 25–80 m. **Diet:** Usually found on sea fans on which they probably feed. **Notes:** Sought-after as collectors' items in Jeffreys Bay, where they are known as 'Jam Tarts'.

Phenacovolva aurantia
Family Ovulidae (False Cowries)

Rare
25 mm

Description: This shell is similar to *P. brevirostris* but is more cylindrical, and has extremities of equal length, which are sculptured by fine oblique striae. The aperture is narrow posteriorly but much wider anteriorly. The body whorl is smooth. **Colour:** White to orange or red on body whorl. Extremities are pale or orange. Outer lip is always white with distinctive pink or orange blotches. **Habitat:** Infratidal, on deep reefs. **Diet:** Probably feeds on sea fans. **Notes:** These shells are sought-after collectors' items.

Volva kilburni
Family Ovulidae (False Cowries)

Rare
60 mm

Description: A relatively large, bulb-shaped shell that is inflated and thick-walled with short, slender and straight extremities. The wide aperture is curved, and is widest at the anterior end. The body whorl is crossed by fine striae. **Colour:** Pink. Outer lip and base are white. **Habitat:** Inhabits deeper water down to 100 m or more. **Diet:** Probably feeds on soft corals and sea fans. **Notes:** These shells occasionally wash up on beaches in the eastern Cape.

Cypraea edentula
Family Cypraeidae (Cowries)

Common
25 mm

Description: A pyriform shell with a sunken spire. The protoconch is not obscured by callus. The dorsum is smooth and the outer lip may have crenulations along the inner edge. **Colour:** Orange and buff to brown, speckled with brown spots. A single brown blotch may be present. Base is white, margins are spotted. **Habitat:** Live specimens are rare, occurring only infratidally. Empty shells abound in beach-drift. **Diet:** Probably feeds on sponges. **Notes:** Due to variation in colour patterns, many subspecies have been named.

Cypraea fuscodentata
Family Cypraeidae (Cowries)

Common
35 mm

Description: This shell has variable forms: it is usually elongate or pyriform. Deep-water forms are globular. The spire is sunken and the dorsum is smooth except for faint transverse striae. Coarse, evenly spaced teeth extend across the outer lip. Coarse riblets cover the entire basal callus. **Colour:** Pale grey, speckled and mottled with brown. Teeth are dark brown but may be colourless. **Habitat:** Infratidal, down to about 130 m. Beach shells are common. **Diet:** Probably feeds on black sponges. **Notes:** This shell is called the 'Giant Owl' in Jeffreys Bay.

Cypraea capensis
Family Cypraeidae (Cowries)

Common
32 mm

Description: An oblong, pyriform or cylindrical shell with a sunken spire that is crossed by fine threads. Regular transverse thread-like striae cross the dorsum. Evenly-spaced denticles on the outer lip continue as fine striae over the dorsum, and end on the columella within the aperture as fine, ridge-like teeth. **Colour:** Mauve to beige with irregular dark brown blotches on dorsum. **Habitat:** Infratidal. Beach shells are common. **Diet:** Herbivorous, grazes on sponges. **Notes:** Interbreeding by *C. capensis* and *C. edentula* resulted in a species called *C. amphitalis*.

Cypraea citrina
Family Cypraeidae (Cowries)

Uncommon
25 mm

Description: A pyriform shell that may be dorsally humped. The spire is elevated. The outer lip has denticles, and is angular and pitted along the upper edge. The base has rounded margins. **Colour:** Dorsum is pale orange to light brown with white spots. Mantle-line is pronounced. Base and margins are glossy orange-brown. Left side of base marked by a long, diffuse brown blotch. **Habitat:** Low-tide edge, down to about 180 m. **Diet:** Probably feeds on sponges. **Notes:** These shells are frequently found in the stomachs of slinger fish.

Cypraea chinensis
Family Cypraeidae (Cowries)

Uncommon
32 mm

Description: A pyriform to globular shell. The spire is obscured by callus and the dorsum is smooth. The denticles on the outer lip are widely spaced. The columellar teeth are weaker, and extend into the aperture. The margins are rounded and project halfway up the sides. **Colour:** Dorsum is bluish white with dark brown speckles. Base and margins are buff, spotted with violet. Teeth are white with orange intervals. **Habitat:** Under rocks from the infratidal fringe downwards. **Diet:** Herbivorous. **Notes:** A deformed form, referred to as *C. chinensis* fm. *tortirostris*, exists.

Cypraea vitellus
Family Cypraeidae (Cowries)

Uncommon
48 mm

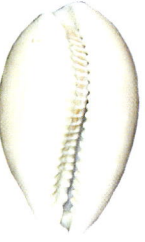

Description: An oval to pyriform shell with a sunken spire, which is completely covered by callus. The margins and base are rounded by strong teeth on the outer lip and columella. **Colour:** Dorsum is fawn to dark brown with white spots of varying sizes. Two to three indistinct transverse bands. Sides have fine streaks. Base is white, fawn or pale lilac. Teeth are white. **Habitat:** Infratidal, extreme low-tide pools and gulleys. **Diet:** Probably feeds on tunicates. **Notes:** It is called the 'Deer Cowry' due to the fawn colour and white spots.

Cypraea moneta
Family Cypraeidae (Cowries)

Rare
24 mm

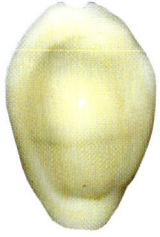 

Description: This shell is variable in shape: oval, angular, flat or humped with thick margins marked by low blunt nodules. The spire is totally covered with callus. **Colour:** Dorsum is bright yellow to greyish white, crossed by two to three grey bands. A bright orange ring is present in some shells. Base and coarse teeth are white. Beach-worn shells are dark purple on the dorsum. **Habitat:** In shallow pools, under rocks. **Diet:** Grazes on algae. **Notes:** Shells were used as a form of currency. Although rare in South Africa, it is the most abundant cowry in other parts of the world.

Cypraea annulus
Family Cypraeidae (Cowries)

Common
24 mm

 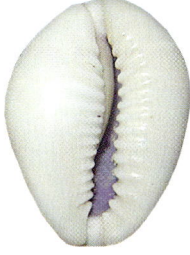

Description: A small, heavy, squat shell with fairly thick margins. The spire is completely covered by callus and the teeth are prominent. **Colour:** Dorsum is bluish grey or light brown, encircled by a bright orange ring. Fine dark lines mark the centre of the dorsum. Base and aperture are white. Dorsum in beach worn shells is a very dark purple. **Habitat:** Infratidal; in rock pools in the intertidal region, may be completely exposed. **Diet:** Grazes on algae. **Notes:** The bright orange ring is a diagnostic feature.

Cypraea helvola
Family Cypraeidae (Cowries)

Common
25 mm

 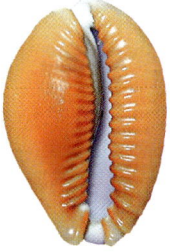

Description: An oval shell that is elliptical and depressed in shape. The spire is covered by callus. The margins are angular and pitted along the upper edges. The teeth are coarse. **Colour:** Dorsum is beige to bluish grey, densely blotched with brown and numerous small white dots. Sides are dark brown, base is orange brown. Terminal areas are lilac and the mantle line is prominent. **Habitat:** Intertidal rock pools, infratidally. **Diet:** Grazes on algae. **Notes:** These shells wash up regularly on KwaZulu-Natal beaches, often in very good condition.

Cypraea erosa
Family Cypraeidae (Cowries)

Common
28 mm

Description: The shell shape is cylindrical and oval. The margin of the outer lip and anterior and posterior ends of columellar margin are prominent with pitted upper borders. Coarse teeth extend to the margin of the inner lip. **Colour:** Dorsum is olive-brown with small white spots, some encircled by brown rings. Spots and streaks occur on the margins, the base is white. **Habitat:** Intertidal under rocks, and infratidally. **Diet:** Mainly algae. **Notes:** The large brown blotch on the side of the shell distinguishes it from all other cowries.

Cypraea caputserpentis
Family Cypraeidae (Cowries)

Common
35 mm

Description: An elliptical, depressed and humped shell with a flat base and angular margins. The spire is completely obscured and the teeth are coarse. **Colour:** Dorsum is chocolate-brown with white to cream spots. Sides are chocolate-brown, becoming pale to white on the base with a white aperture. Grey to light brown terminal blotches occur dorsally. **Habitat:** Mostly intertidally under rocks in pools, may be completely exposed. **Diet:** Mainly algae. **Notes:** Mostly only emerges at night to graze.

Cypraea arabica immanis
Family Cypraeidae (Cowries)

Common
80 mm

Description: A heavy shell with a rounded, bulging dorsum. The margins are angular. The spire is raised and prominent. **Colour:** Dorsum is light brown with fawn blotches, overlaid by dark brown axial lines and spots. Margins are grey with large dark brown spots, base is light orange to reddish brown. Teeth are dark brown. **Habitat:** Low-tide level in pools under rocks and in crevices, often in pairs. **Diet:** Omnivorous, feeds on algae and small marine organisms. **Notes:** The South African form (*immanis*) is larger than those from the rest of their range.

Cypraea tigris
Family Cypraeidae (Cowries)

Uncommon
105 mm

Description: This heavy shell is the largest cowry in the region. It has an inflated shape and rounded margins. The sunken spire is obscured by callus. **Colour:** Dorsum is grey, bluish grey, buff or brown mottled with black or dark brown spots. Base and teeth are white. The mantle line is usually uniformly brown. **Habitat:** On sand and on rocks in deep pools, often in the open. **Diet:** Feeds on sponges. **Notes:** This species is rare in South Africa but common in Mozambique. Often found in pairs.

Cypraea histrio
Family Cypraeidae (Cowries)

Rare
62 mm

Description: A humped shell with steep sides and rounded margins. The callus obscures the raised spire. **Colour:** The cream to bluish-grey dorsum is crossed by a dark brown band, overlaid by brownish reticulations, resulting in round or straight-sided spots. Sides are bluish grey to cream with large dark brown spots. Base is cream, teeth are dark brown. Extremities have fawn dorsal terminal blotches. **Habitat:** Intertidal pools under rocks, infratidally. **Diet:** Grazes on algae. **Notes:** Rare in South Africa. Common in Mozambique and further north.

Semicassis labiata zeylanica
Family Cassidae (Helmet Shells)

Common
65 mm

Description: A heavy, oblong, inflated shell with a smooth outer lip and concave spire whorls. The exterior is marked by one to three rows of prominent peripheral nodules. The callus is extensive. The operculum is small and smooth. **Colour:** Light brown to purplish brown with three to five rows of large white spots. Outer lip is flecked with dark brown. **Habitat:** In sheltered low-tide pools with sandy bottoms. Infratidally. **Diet:** Feeds on pansy shells (*Echinodiscus bisperforatus*). **Notes:** Prominent peripheral nodules distinguish this species from *S. l. iredalei*.

Semicassis labiata iredalei
Family Cassidae (Helmet Shells)

Common
55 mm

Description: A globular shell that may appear almost cylindrical. The short spire is raised. Suppressed nodules occur on the exterior, forming low ridges. The subsutural area is concave. **Colour:** Light yellowish brown, dark brown to purple-brown with rows of white spots. Outer lip has paired dark brown spots. Interior is purplish brown. **Habitat:** Low-tide gulleys and rock pools in coarse sand. Infratidal. **Diet:** Feeds on sea urchins. **Notes:** Drills holes through the shell of the prey by means of a radula.

Phalium areola
Family Cassidae (Helmet Shells)

Common
65 mm

Description: An oblong, inflated shell with a glossy and smooth exterior. The high, sharp spire has concave sides, sculptured by axial and spiral ribs, and two to four varices. Spiral grooves mark the body whorl. The outer lip is thickened with sharp teeth and the columella shield carries strong folds. A narrow, rounded varix is present next to the columella. **Colour:** White to buff with five rows of dark brown, square blotches, also on lip. **Habitat:** Infratidal. **Diet:** Predator of gastropods and bivalves. **Notes:** An aberrant form is frequently washed ashore.

Phalium fimbria
Family Cassidae (Helmet Shells)

Rare
80 mm

Description: A heavy, elongate shell, sculptured by well-developed rounded axial ridges that form points at the shoulder, and become obsolete towards the anterior end. The short, pointed spire is marked by three to four varices. The body whorl is large and the aperture narrow. A strong varix occurs behind the outer lip. The columella shield is extensive, columella is ridged. **Colour:** Yellowish white with wavy yellowish-brown axial bands. Brown blotches occur on outer lip. **Habitat:** Infratidal. **Diet:** Predator of molluscs and worms. **Notes:** Whole shells are a rare find.

Cypraecassis rufa
Family Cassidae (Helmet Shells)

Uncommon
120 mm

Description: A large, heavy shell sculptured by three to four knobbed spiral bands with weaker intermediate spiral ridges. The aperture is long and narrow. The outer lip protrudes above the short and depressed spire and the parietal callus is large and sharply demarcated at the outer edge. Nodules are replaced by numerous coarse axial ridges towards the anterior end. Spiral ridges cross the axial ridges, separating them into short segments. **Colour:** Mottled reddish brown with lighter blotches. **Habitat:** Infratidal near coral reefs in sand. **Diet:** Feeds on molluscs and sea urchins. **Notes:** Used for cameo carving.

Tonna variegata
Family Tonnidae (Tun Shells)

Uncommon
70 mm

Description: An oval, globular and thin shell with a low spire and a deep suture. The outer lip is ridged. The columella base is twisted and the columella shield has a thick callus. The umbilicus is deep. Sculpture of broad spiral cords with much weaker intermediate ridges. **Colour:** Light to reddish brown, with white blotches and dark brown bars or chevrons. **Habitat:** In shallow water on sandy bottoms. **Diet:** Feeds on sea cucumbers. **Notes:** *T. variegata* fm. *dunkeri* is smaller, heavier and darker, with a thick parietal callus. Known in Jeffreys Bay as 'Boxing Gloves'.

Tonna perdix

Family Tonnidae (Tun Shells)

Uncommon
100 mm

Description: An elongate, oval and thin shell with a high, fairly sharp spire. The suture is moderately deep, and the shoulders slope markedly. The umbilicus is narrow and deep. Strong flat spiral ribs contain shallow intermediate grooves. The parietal callus is thin and the columella base is twisted towards the aperture. **Colour:** Shell is cream; spiral ribs are brown, interrupted by white axial streaks. Outer lip is white inside and has a brown inner edge. **Habitat:** Offshore on sand. **Diet:** Feeds on sea cucumbers. **Notes:** Spire often broken in collected shells.

Ficus ficus

Family Ficidae (Fig Shells)

Uncommon
80 mm

Description: A globular shell with a low spire, long siphonal canal and convex whorls. The shoulder is rounded and the aperture wide. The outer lip is smooth and thin. Weaker and stronger spiral ridges are crossed by fine axial ridges. **Colour:** Light brown, flecked with darker brown. Paler spiral bands with reddish-brown blotches on body whorl. Aperture is violet to brown. **Habitat:** Sheltered areas along low-tide fringes to deeper water. **Diet:** Primarily sand-dwelling worms. **Notes:** Although the shell is drab, the living animal is colourful.

Bursa granularis
Family Bursidae (Frog Shells)

Common
58 mm

Description: A compressed shell with a sharp, high spire, sculptured by spiral rows of increasingly bigger nodules. Two varices occur on the body whorl and spire. The large aperture has denticles on the inner edge of the outer lip. Transverse ridges mark the columella. **Colour:** Reddish brown. Paler bands occur on body whorl and varices. **Habitat:** Lower intertidal zone on rocks. **Diet:** Feeds on molluscs, worms, scavenges dead animal matter. **Notes:** *B. granularis* has fine granules, *B. g.* fm. *alfredensis* is without granules, and *B. g.* fm. *affinis* has coarse, rounded nodules.

Bursa rosa
Family Bursidae (Frog Shells)

Uncommon
45 mm

Description: A compressed shell with a high spire. The small aperture has a projecting anal canal. Projections are also retained on the earlier whorls. The siphonal canal is reflected and deflected from the axis. The varices are thick and rough. The outer lip has strong, paired teeth. The columella has a few transverse ridges. Rough spiral ridges are marked by strong peripheral nodules. **Colour:** Cream to buff, dotted with brown. Aperture is purple. **Habitat:** Low-tide pools and under rocks. **Diet:** Feeds on worms and other molluscs. **Notes:** Easily recognized by the chimney-like projections.

Bursa bufonia
Family Bursidae (Frog Shells)

Uncommon

50 mm

Description: A squat, heavy and compressed shell with a raised spire. The outer lip bears ridge-like teeth and the columella has weak pleats. The anal canal is spout-like – similar spouts are retained on the earlier whorls. The siphonal canal is short and deflected from the axial line. Two varices occur on each whorl. Spiral ridges form large nodules at the periphery of each whorl. **Colour:** Cream with a reddish-brown tint on varices and spiral ridges. **Habitat:** Infratidal, in low-tide pools under rocks. **Diet:** Preys on worms and molluscs. **Notes:** Juveniles may be confused with *B. rosa*.

Bufonaria crumena
Family Bursidae (Frog Shells)

Common

70 mm

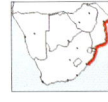
Description: A thin, compressed shell with strong varices on either side of the aperture extending up the sides of the spire. The outer lip has denticles. Sculpture of spiral and beaded ridges. Row of tubercles occurs on the shoulder of each whorl, three occur on the body whorl. **Colour:** Light brown. Tubercles are pale; brown streaks between tubercles. Varices are brown. Aperture is white, outer lip marked with yellow. **Habitat:** Infratidal down to 50 m, on sand or mud among submerged rocks in sheltered areas. **Diet:** Feeds on worms. **Notes:** Shells in good condition seldom wash ashore.

Tutufa bubo
Family Bursidae (Frog Shells)

Uncommon
200 mm

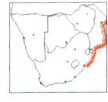

Description: A large, thick, heavy shell with an inflated body whorl and a raised spire. The shell has a deep anal canal and a broad, short siphonal canal. The outer lip is thick with rounded ridges extending into the aperture. The columella is flared, and has a few weak folds. The spiral cords are prominent and have large nodules on the periphery of the whorls. Two varices occur on each whorl. **Colour:** Cream to white, flecked with brown spots and lines. Aperture is cream to orange. **Habitat:** Mainly infratidal on coral sand. **Diet:** Predator of worms. **Notes:** The shells are often encrusted with marine growth.

Charonia lampas pustulata
Family Ranellidae (Tritons)

Common
200 mm

Description: The adult shell is large, heavy and thick. The spire is high and sharp but usually eroded. The whorls are strongly shouldered with spiral nodules and numerous spiral ridges. Strong varices. The outer lip has 10–12 ridge-like teeth, while the columella is marked by low transverse ridges. **Colour:** Dull buff, blotched with brown. Light and dark blotches on spiral ridges. Outer lip is brown on the ridges. **Habitat:** Infratidal, in intertidal rock pools. **Diet:** Carnivorous, preying on sea urchins and starfish. **Notes:** The animal is reddish pink and valued as bait; known as the 'Pink Lady'.

Cabestana cutacea

Family Ranellidae (Tritons)

Common
80 mm

Description: A short, oval shell with a high spire, which may be short or elongate. The outer lip has paired rounded teeth, and the inner lip is smooth. The umbilicus is narrow and deep and the siphonal canal is short. Varices are strong or absent. Two forms occur: the first form has strong spiral cords, fine axial striae and low axial ribs. The second form has rounded nodules, flattened spiral ridges and fine axial striae. **Colour:** Brown, reddish brown to orange. **Habitat:** Infratidal among ascidians. Low-tide level. **Diet:** Probably preys on ascidians. **Notes:** Intergrading between forms is common.

Cymatium parthenopium

Family Ranellidae (Tritons)

Common
110 mm

Description: A heavy shell with a long spire and a short siphonal canal. The outer lip has paired coarse teeth, while the inner lip has irregular, transverse ridges. Angular cords with coarse nodules occur in the shoulder region. **Colour:** Light brown. Varices and outside of outer lip are brown and white. Aperture is white inside. Outer lip is salmon; teeth are white. Interstices are dark brown. Inner lip is dark brown and the ridges are white. **Habitat:** Intertidal among rocks, infratidally. **Diet:** Preys on bivalves and probably gastropods. **Notes:** Thick, fibrous, matted periostracum facilitates identification.

Cymatium pileare

Family Ranellidae (Tritons)

Common
90 mm

Description: An elongate, narrow shell with a high spire and strong varices. The siphonal canal is short and slightly curved. The outer lip has small, paired denticles which continue as rounded ridges, while the inner lip has numerous plicae. The exterior is sculptured by beaded spiral cords and fine axial striae. **Colour:** Reddish brown with darker bands. Pale peripheral band. Varices are white and dark brown. Aperture is red with white ridges. Periostracum is brown and thick. **Habitat:** Infratidal, in crevices in low-tide pools. **Diet:** Carnivorous. **Notes:** Shell is narrower than *C. parthenopium*.

Cymatium aquatile

Family Ranellidae (Tritons)

Uncommon
65 mm

Description: An elongate shell with a high spire that is shorter than in *C. pileare*. The siphonal canal is slightly curved. The outer lip has two rows of paired denticles, while the inner lip has numerous ridges. Coarse nodules occur on the exterior. **Colour:** Light brown, lighter band occurs below periphery of body whorl. Varices are white and dark brown. Aperture is flesh-coloured, inner lip is brown, ridges are white. Periostracum is brown and hairy. **Habitat:** Mainly infratidal. Intertidal at low-tide level in rock pools. **Diet:** Preys on molluscs, worms, starfish and sea urchins. **Notes:** The outer lip is characteristic.

Cymatium closeli
Family Ranellidae (Tritons)

Common
40 mm

Description: An elongate shell with a high spire marked with varices. The outer lip has denticles that continue as ridges into the aperture, while the inner lip is ridged. The siphonal canal is narrow. Intermediate striae of the spiral ridges are crossed by axial ribs, rendering them granular. **Colour:** Reddish brown. Varices are dark brown with white streaks. Orange at base of denticles. Inner lip is orange-red with white ridges. **Habitat:** Mostly infratidal. Low-tide pools. **Diet:** Feeds on molluscs, worms and sea urchins. **Notes:** Although common, it is popular with collectors.

Ranella australasia gemmifera
Family Ranellidae (Tritons)

Uncommon
90 mm

Description: An elongate shell with a high spire and convex whorls. The siphonal canal is short. Weak denticles occur on the outer lip; the columella is smooth. One nodule occurs in the parietal region. Nodules occur on the exterior periphery. Sculpture of fine spiral striae, sometimes low spiral ridges. The varix is raised on one side. **Colour:** Dark to reddish brown with lighter marks on varices. Outer lip is white with dark brown bars. **Habitat:** In sand in low-tide pools among rocks, in gulleys. **Diet:** Feeds on reef-worms. **Notes:** Animal secretes acid saliva, which dissolves the worm's tube, paralysing and dissolving the worm.

Argobuccinum pustulosum

Family Ranellidae (Tritons)

Common

90 mm

Description: A compressed, squat shell. The siphonal canal is short and straight. The thick outer lip has weak teeth and the blunt, inner lip has an elongate nodule in parietal region. Sculptured by fine spiral striae, low spiral ridges with rounded nodules and fine axial striae. **Colour:** Reddish brown with dark brown nodular bands, aperture is white. Periostracum is greenish brown. **Habitat:** Infratidal. Among rocks in low-tide pools. **Diet:** Feeds on reef-worms. **Notes:** Western Cape specimens are narrower, and have a higher spire, with smaller nodules than those to the east.

Gyrineum pusillum

Family Ranellidae (Tritons)

Common

24 mm

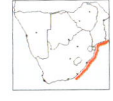

Description: A small, laterally compressed shell with a short siphonal canal. The outer lip has weak teeth, while the inner lip has folds at the base. Sculptured by spiral ridges and axial riblets, forming granules where they intersect. An oblique, fin-like varix is present on either side of the spire. **Colour:** Cream, yellow or bluish grey with bands of purplish brown below the suture. Aperture is purple. **Habitat:** Intertidal, in low-tide pools. **Diet:** Preys on small worms and marine creatures. **Notes:** *G. cuspidataeformis* is similar but has fewer axial ribs.

Distorsio anus
Family Personidae (Distorsios)

Rare
50 mm

Description: An oval, fusiform shell with a moderately raised spire that has irregular whorls. The outer lip is flat and expanded with two rows of denticles. The large columella shield has a thin, plate-like extension along the margin; prominent folds and pustules. The aperture is irregular and narrowed by teeth, nodules and folds. **Colour:** Spiral and axial cords are white with brown bands and blotches. Columella and outer lip are white. **Habitat:** Mainly infratidal, particularly on coral reefs. Low-tide pools under rocks. **Diet:** Predatory. Diet is unknown. **Notes:** Largest species of the family.

Gyroscala coronata
Family Epitoniidae (Wenteltraps)

Common
32 mm

Description: A light shell with a high tapering spire that has convex whorls. A thin spiral thread encircles the base. The umbilicus is closed. The exterior surface is sculptured by about 12–16 raised lamellae that are indented at the suture. **Colour:** White. Brown spiral line below suture continues on to the base. Short brown spiral lines present on the periphery of whorls, which is evident in juveniles. **Habitat:** Low-tide pools under rocks, in sand. Shells often wash up with seaweeds. **Diet:** Presumably feeds on sea anemones. **Notes:** Known as 'Dresdens' in Jeffreys Bay.

Gyroscala lamellosa
Family Epitoniidae (Wenteltraps)

Common
28 mm

Description: This shell may be confused with *G. coronata*. The whorls are more straight-sided and the spire is high and pointed. The axial lamellae are fairly thick, numbering about 9–11, and are not indented at the suture. **Colour:** Two colour forms can be distinguished: The first is a white form with a brown line immediately below, or at, the suture. The second form is brown with white lamellae. **Habitat:** Infratidal. Low-tide pools among sea anemones, in sand under rocks. **Diet:** Presumably sea anemones. **Notes:** Also known as 'Dresdens'.

Architectonica gualtierii
Family Architectonicidae (Sundials)

Uncommon
45 mm

Description: A depressed shell with convex whorls containing three spiral grooves. The four spiral ridges have axial striae on the dorsum. The base has four shallow grooves. A prominent ridge occurs at the perimeter, followed by a weaker ridge, a plicate flat area and a nodular cord. A denticulate ridge encircles the umbilicus. **Colour:** Brown with reddish-brown and white blotches. Apex is mauve. Umbilicus and denticles are light brown. **Habitat:** Infratidal. Low-tide fringe. **Diet:** Feeds on corals and sea anemones. **Notes:** Live shells often found lying on dorsum, revealing wide umbilicus.

Architectonica perspectiva

Family Architectonicidae (Sundials)

Uncommon
40 mm

Description: A depressed shell with convex whorls. The suture is deep and followed by a narrow ridge. **Colour:** Concentric markings begin with a continuous brown line on ridge, followed by a white granular band, a second brown ridge, a broad band of light colour and a narrow ridge dotted with brown and white. Base has three spotted ridges, a plicate fawn area, a nodular ridge and a brownish denticulate ridge running into the umbilicus. **Habitat:** Infratidal, to 50 m. **Diet:** Feeds on corals, zooanthids and sea anemones. **Notes:** Appear to be hermaphrodites.

Janthina janthina

Family Janthinidae (Purple Sea Snails)

Common
35 mm

Description: The shell width is greater than the shell height. A depressed shell with a large aperture. The spire is low with convex whorls. The inflated body whorl has a rounded peripheral angle. A shallow notch occurs on the margin of the outer lip; the columella is twisted. Sculptured by fine growth-lines and spiral grooves. **Colour:** Light lavender or violet-white above the peripheral angle, dark purple on base. **Habitat:** Pelagic, hanging upside-down from a raft of mucus-coated bubbles. **Diet:** Feeds on jelly fish, crustaceans and zooplankton. **Notes:** Young are born as veliger larvae.

Janthina prolongata
Family Janthinidae (Purple Sea Snails)

Common
35 mm

Description: A globular shell with a large aperture. The spire is low with numerous folds; the suture is deep. The body whorl is large and has a rounded periphery. The outer lip has a short spout on the base and a rounded notch. The umbilicus is narrow and partly covered by the reflected columella. The exterior has growth-lines, which meet at the periphery of the body whorl. **Colour:** Pale violet to purple. **Habitat:** Pelagic, hanging upside-down from a raft of mucus-coated bubbles. **Diet:** Preys on jelly fish, crustaceans and zooplankton. **Notes:** Animals wash up in large numbers with *J. janthina* and blue bottles after storms.

Murex brevispina
Family Muricidae (Murex Shells)

Uncommon
75 mm

Description: A globular, inflated shell with a low spire and shouldered whorls. The outer lip has ridge-like teeth and the columellar edge is raised. The siphonal canal is long and narrow. The exterior has three varices that bear three spines. Two axial ridges with rounded tubercles occur between the varices. Short spiral spines mark the siphonal canal. **Colour:** Dull reddish brown. Aperture is yellowish brown, white columella. **Habitat:** Low-tide fringe buried in sandy mud. **Diet:** Feeds on molluscs and barnacles. **Notes:** Animals are communal spawners. Form huge mass of egg capsules from which veligers hatch.

Chicoreus ramosus
Family Muricidae (Murex Shells)

Uncommon
200 mm

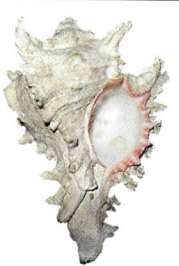

Description: A large, heavy shell with an inflated body whorl. The siphonal canal is curved and flattened. The outer lip has teeth – one tooth is large. The columellar edge is raised. Three prominent varices occur per whorl, and are strongly fronded with recurved shoulder spines and with intervals of one major and two minor axial ridges. **Colour:** Light brown, outer lip and columella are pink. **Habitat:** Inter- and infratidal, in rubble, stones and sand. **Diet:** Preys on gastropods, particularly bivalves. **Notes:** KwaZulu-Natal specimens are much more uncommon and smaller than those from Mozambique.

Chicoreus austramosus
Family Muricidae (Murex Shells)

Uncommon
50 mm

Description: This shell is smaller than *C. ramosus*. The whorls are strongly shouldered and the spire is high and angular. The outer lip has teeth and two fronds at the base. The columella does not have a raised edge. The exterior has thick varices with folded fronds, the one on the shoulder is prominent. Intervals have two strong nodules, and spiral threads and granules. Two spines occur on the siphonal canal. **Colour:** Buff cream to pink, aperture is white. **Habitat:** Infratidal. **Diet:** Preys on molluscs and bivalves. **Notes:** Worn shells wash up on the beach. Fresh shells are collected by divers, or are found in fish stomachs.

Pteropurpura uncinaria

Family Muricidae (Murex Shells)

Uncommon
24 mm

Description: A small, angular shell with a fairly high spire. The oval aperture and the closed siphonal canal form a tube. The outer lip and columella are smooth and the columella edge is raised. The exterior has three varices per whorl. The shoulder spine is prominent and curved upwards, and does not touch the spines above. The minor spines, four of which occur on the base of the body whorl, are short, erect and tubercle-like. **Colour:** Cream to brown. **Habitat:** Infratidal. **Diet:** Feeds on other gastropods and barnacles. **Notes:** Known as the 'Stag' or 'Takbok' in Jeffreys Bay.

Pteropurpura graagae

Family Muricidae (Murex Shells)

Common
20 mm

Description: This small shell is narrower than *P. uncinaria*. The spire is high and the suture deep. Three varices occur on the body whorl. The spines curve towards the apex and touch the previous spine of the whorl above. One row of spines occurs on the edge of the aperture. Five to six minor comb-like spines or tubercles curve upwards on the base of the body whorl. **Colour:** White to grey to reddish brown. **Habitat:** Under loose rocks in low-tide pools, in gulleys. **Diet:** Feeds on small gastropods and barnacles. **Notes:** Spines on body whorl are a diagnostic feature.

Drupa ricinus
Family Muricidae (Murex Shells)

Common
28 mm

Description: A squat, globular shell with a low spire and a narrow, long aperture. The thick outer lip has two grooved teeth, while the columella has two to three ridge-like teeth. Sculptured by five spiral rows of spines, the longest spines project from the aperture edge. Weak spiral threads occur in intervals. **Colour:** Cream, tips of spines are dark brown or black. Aperture is white with an orange line around margin. **Habitat:** Intertidal, in rock pools. **Diet:** Feeds on sponges, barnacles and molluscs. **Notes:** The white-lipped *D. r. albolabris* occurs in northern KwaZulu-Natal and Mozambique.

Drupa morum
Family Muricidae (Murex Shells)

Uncommon
44 mm

Description: A moderately large, thick and globular shell with a short spire. The body whorl is large, the base flat and the aperture is narrow. The outer lip has two fused and two single teeth. The columella has three to four folds. Four spiral rows of large, blunt or conical nodes occur on the body whorl. **Colour:** Buff with black nodes. Aperture is dark violet with lighter teeth and columellar teeth. **Habitat:** Intertidal on rocks, but difficult to find as it is usually covered by marine growth. **Diet:** Feeds on worms, sponges, barnacles and other molluscs. **Notes:** Recognized by its purple aperture.

Morula granulata

Family Muricidae (Murex Shells)

Abundant
24 mm

Description: A thick, biconical shell with a high spire. The aperture is narrow. The outer lip has two strong teeth and a few weaker ones. The columella is smooth with basal granules. Spiral rows of rounded tubercles occur on the body whorl and on the spire. **Colour:** Greyish white with dark brown to black tubercles, outer lip is black. Aperture and columella are bluish grey. Often eroded. **Habitat:** Upper mid-tidal zone. **Diet:** Carnivorous, feeding on molluscs and barnacles. **Notes:** Known as mulberry shell. This species influences the abundance of oysters by preying on newly settled juveniles.

Cronia ochrostoma

Family Muricidae (Murex Shells)

Common
26 mm

Description: A biconical shell with a sharp, conical spire. The body whorl is inflated and the aperture is narrow. The outer lip is ridged inside. The columella has a few weak granules. Four strong spiral ridges occur on the body whorl. Five scaly striae are present in intervals. The prominent axial ribs have sharp nodules where they cross the spiral ridges. **Colour:** White to buff cream, brown tinge on axial ribs evident in juveniles. Aperture is yellow, base of columella is white. **Habitat:** Mid-tidal pools. **Diet:** Preys on other molluscs, eats dead animal matter. **Notes:** Encrusted with marine growth and calcium deposits.

Cronia margariticola
Family Muricidae (Murex Shells)

Common
36 mm

Description: A squat shell with a sharp, conical spire. The shoulder is moderately prominent and the outer lip bears small teeth. Sculptured by strong axial ribs, which are crossed by numerous spiral threads forming tubercles at the intersections. The spiral threads are crossed by crinkly growth-lines, resulting in a densely scaled appearance. **Colour:** Dark brown to black with paler spiral bands. Aperture is brownish purple. **Habitat:** Shallow pools in upper mid-tidal zone. **Diet:** Scavenger, also preys on molluscs. **Notes:** Older shells are usually eroded and encrusted.

Mancinella alouina
Family Muricidae (Murex Shells)

Uncommon
50 mm

Description: A thick, oval shell with a low and concave spire. The aperture is wide, the siphonal canal is short and the outer lip bears teeth. Sculpture of close spiral threads. Four to five rows of spiny nodules occur on the body whorl and are stronger towards the outer lip. **Colour:** Light to reddish brown. Purplish-brown to pale brown nodules. Aperture and columella are bright yellow with orange or reddish lines running into aperture. **Habitat:** Intertidal reefs, in sheltered pools or gulleys. **Diet:** Preys on molluscs and tubeworms. **Notes:** Lines in aperture are diagnostic.

Mancinella echinulata Common
Family Muricidae (Murex Shells)   45 mm

Description: A heavy, oval shell with a low spire. The outer lip has small teeth and a few thin spiral lines. The columella bears weak pleats. The exterior is marked by fine spiral lines forming four rows of blunt nodules, which are less prominent than in *M. alouina*. **Colour:** Light brown to creamy brown. Inner margin of outer lip and columella are orange; interior is white. **Habitat:** Exposed rocks in the intertidal zone. **Diet:** Drills holes into mussels to devour them. **Notes:** In Zululand, this species is common and is found in the crevices at the top of rocky outcrops.

Purpura panama Common
Family Muricidae (Rock Shells)   60 mm

Description: A heavy, squat shell with a moderately short spire. The siphonal canal is short and wide; the anal canal is distinct. The outer lip has small teeth, and the columella is concave. Sculpture of numerous, close, flat, spiral ridges that bear large tubercles. The shoulder on the body whorl is low and rounded. **Colour:** Dark brown, black and grey. Aperture is dark brown on inside margin of outer lip. Bluish grey inside aperture. Columella is orange. **Habitat:** Mid-tidal rock pools. **Diet:** Drills into barnacles and oysters. **Notes:** Females aggregate to deposit their egg capsules.

Thais bufo
Family Muricidae (Rock Shells)

Common
60 mm

Description: A heavy, squat shell with a low spire. The siphonal canal is short and the anal canal is well developed. The outer lip has ridge-like teeth. The columella is rounded with a heavy deposit of callus anterior to the anal canal. Sculpture of numerous flat spiral ridges bearing four rows of blunt, rounded tubercles. **Colour:** Dark brown to grey. Margin of outer lip has brown streaks. Aperture and columella are orange. **Habitat:** Rock pools and crevices. **Diet:** Feeds on barnacles and oysters. **Notes:** These molluscs may occur side by side over a distance of a metre or two.

Thais capensis
Family Muricidae (Rock Shells)

Common
70 mm

Description: A moderately large, heavy shell with a raised spire. The whorls are shouldered, and the shoulder slope is concave. The outer lip has small teeth, and the columella is smooth and rounded. Sculptured by four rows of strong, blunt tubercles. Fine spiral striae. **Colour:** Generally grey or buff with areas of brown. Aperture with brown bands visible from inside. Columella and interior are yellow or salmon. **Habitat:** Infratidal. Low neap-tide pools under rocks, in crevices and gulleys. **Diet:** Preys on gastropods and ascidians. **Notes:** Animals are communal spawners of masses of egg capsules.

Nucella dubia
Family Muricidae (Murex Shells)

Common
40 mm

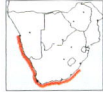

Description: A shell that is variable in form, colour, size and habitat. The whorls are convex, the spire fairly short and the columella flattened. Sculptured by numerous flattened, unequal spiral threads and irregular growth-lines. **Colour:** Grey, or reddish brown with dark brown to black spiral bands, spots, blotches, and including wavy or zigzag axial bands of black and white markings. **Habitat:** Exposed rocks in crevices, under loose stones from high-tide to low neap-tide levels. **Diet:** Preys on limpets, barnacles and littorines. **Notes:** A small form *N. d.* fm. *acutispira* occurs in the same distribution range.

Nucella cingulata
Family Muricidae (Murex Shells)

Common
38 mm

Description: An oval shell with a raised spire and angular whorls. The outer lip is denticulate or grooved, corresponding with the external ridges. Sculptured by high spiral cords, varying in number from one to six. Smooth shells without cords also occur. **Colour:** Creamy-white to dark brown. Aperture is orange-brown to almost chocolate-brown with lighter bands corresponding to external ridges. **Habitat:** Infratidal down to 20 m. Among mussels at low-tide level. **Diet:** Drills holes through the shells of mussels and barnacles. **Notes:** Shells without ridges, or with five or six ridges, are popular.

Nucella squamosa

Family Muricidae (Murex Shells)

Common
50 mm

Description: A globular shell with a raised spire and convex whorls. The short grooves on the outer edge of the outer lip correspond with the external ridges. Sculptured by fine and strong spiral threads that are crossed by irregular axial ribs, giving the shell a cancellate appearance. **Colour:** A brown to reddish-brown shell with darker axial streaks. Outer lip is reddish brown, columella is white. **Habitat:** Infratidal down to about 50 m. Low-tide pools and in gulleys. **Diet:** Preys on molluscs and probably acidians. **Notes:** This shell may be covered with the hydroid *Hydractinia altispina*.

Nassa francolina

Family Muricidae (Murex Shells)

Uncommon
50 mm

Description: An elliptical shell with a low and sharp spire and convex whorls. The aperture is large and elliptical with a weak pleat anteriorly and a strong pleat posteriorly on the inside of the outer lip. The strong parietal nodule is ridge-like. **Colour:** Dark brown with light lavender flecks on periphery and base of body whorl. Inner edge of outer lip is brown, aperture is cream inside, columella is brown to yellowish brown. **Habitat:** Infratidal fringe, living on sand under rocks. **Diet:** Feeds on gastropods. **Notes:** The name *francolina* is derived from Italian, meaning 'partridge'.

Rapana rapiformis   Uncommon
Family Muricidae (Murex Shells)   100 mm

Description: A large and globular shell with a short, sharp and stepped spire and an expanded body whorl. The suture is deep and the aperture large. The wide umbilicus is edged by a broad scaly rim and the outer lip has ridge-like teeth. Sculptured by a spiral row of thick scales or spines, numerous fine spiral striae and axial riblets and weaker rows of scaly nodules on the body whorl. **Colour:** Pale brown, blotched and spotted with darker brown. Aperture is salmon. **Habitat:** Infratidal among corals. **Diet:** Probably preys on soft corals. **Notes:** Rare in South Africa; washes up in poor condition.

Coralliophila fritschi   Common
Family Coralliophilidae (Coral Shells)   25 mm

Description: A narrow shell with a high spire and convex whorls with weak shoulders. The umbilicus is small. The outer lip is smooth inside. The columella is smooth. The exterior has alternately weaker and stronger spiral threads. Threads bear small, dense scales. Axial ribs are rounded, forming a slight shoulder. **Colour:** Off-white in fresh specimens but beach shells are usually light to dark pink. **Habitat:** Infratidal, and often found in association with reef-forming corals. **Diet:** Preys on soft and hard corals, and sea anemones. **Notes:** Called 'Coral Shells' in Jeffreys Bay.

Coralliophila squamosissima Common
Family Coralliophilidae (Coral Shells) 28 mm

Description: A squat, globular shell with a fairly short spire and convex whorls. The body whorl is inflated and the short siphonal canal is deflected. The umbilicus is narrow or closed. Sculptured by fairly strong, scaly, spiral threads with weaker intermediate threads, and crossed by oblique axial ribs, giving the shell a cancellate appearance. **Colour:** White or grey-white, inner aperture is glossy white. **Habitat:** Mainly infratidal among corals and sea fans. **Diet:** Preys on soft corals. **Notes:** Live shells can sometimes be found intertidally on the soft coral *Palythoa nelliae*.

Mipus rosaceus Common
Family Coralliophilidae (Coral Shells) 20 mm

Description: A squat shell. The spire is shorter than in *C. fritschi*. The whorls are convex with a weak peripheral angle and the siphonal canal is short and angled. The umbilicus is very narrow and the outer lip has teeth, with weak ridges occurring inside the aperture. Sculpture of fine spiral threads, which intersect low, rounded axial ribs with rounded nodules at the periphery. **Colour:** Off-white in live gastropods, pink in worn shells. **Habitat:** Infratidal, near coral reefs. **Diet:** Preys on the polyps of corals. **Notes:** These shells are also known as 'Corals' in Jeffreys Bay due to their pink colour.

Volema pyrum
Family Melongenidae (Melongenas)

Uncommon
55 mm

Description: A heavy, pyriform shell with a depressed spire and a sharp, strong shoulder. Weak ridges occur on the outer lip and extend into the aperture. The base has a false umbilicus. The exterior has shallow spiral grooves on the shoulder and on the base. **Colour:** Reddish brown to dark brown or light brown, rarely white. Aperture and columella are yellowish brown to orange- brown. Periostracum is velvety olive-brown. **Habitat:** Burrows in mud and sand flats. **Diet:** Feeds on other molluscs. **Notes:** This species was once common in Durban bay but is now seldom seen.

Afrocominella elongata
Family Buccinidae (Whelks)

Common
50 mm

Description: A fusiform shell with a high, tapering spire. The whorls are weakly shouldered and the siphonal canal is fairly short and angled. The outer lip is ridged along the inner margin. The smooth columella has a parietal tubercle. The exterior is sculptured by rounded spiral ridges that become finer between shoulder and suture. **Colour:** Fawn or cream with reddish-brown axial streaks and patches. **Habitat:** Mainly infratidal down to about 80 m. Under loose rocks in intertidal pools. **Diet:** Probably scavengers. **Notes:** This shell could be confused with *A. turtoni* and *A. capensis*.

Burnupena cincta
Family Buccinidae (Whelks)

Common
58 mm

Description: A fairly heavy shell with a high spire and convex whorls that are frequently eroded. The outer lip is thin, the columella smooth and the siphonal canal is short and wide. Sculptured by strong rounded ridges. The area between the shoulder and the suture is deeply furrowed. **Colour:** Reddish brown with axial streaks of brown. Aperture is white to light violet. Periostracum is brown to greenish brown. **Habitat:** Inhabits rock pools in lower intertidal zone. **Diet:** Scavenger. **Notes:** The shell sculpture of the infratidal species, *B.c.* fm. *semisulcata*, is smooth and has no spiral cords.

Burnupena lagenaria
Family Buccinidae (Whelks)

Common
40 mm

Description: A squat shell with a short spire. The body whorl is large and inflated and the inside of the outer lip is finely ridged. The siphonal canal is short and wide. Sculptured by strong spiral ridges with numerous fine striae in the interspaces. Deep furrows occur above the shoulders of the whorls. **Colour:** Brown, spiral ridges are spotted with white and dark brown; axial streaks are brown. Aperture is light brown, columella is white. Rough periostracum is brown to greenish brown. **Habitat:** Intertidal rock pools and in crevices. **Diet:** Scavenger. **Notes:** This species occasionally intergrades with *B. cincta*.

Burnupena limbosa
Family Buccinidae (Whelks)

Common
50 mm

Description: A pyriform and elongate shell with a high spire and whorls which are convex below the shallow suture. The apex is often worn and the outer lip has weak denticles. The columella is enamelled with a parietal nodule. The siphonal canal is short and wide and the anal canal is deep. Sculptured by fine spiral threads, which are coarser on the base. **Colour:** Brown. Aperture is white to purplish brown. Thick periostracum is dark brown. **Habitat:** Infratidal. Exposed rocks at the spring low-tide level. **Diet:** Scavenger. **Notes:** This shell is similar to *B. papyracea*, but the periostracum is not papery.

Burnupena pubescens
Family Buccinidae (Whelks)

Common
50 mm

Description: An elongate shell with a high spire. The siphonal canal is very short and open. The anal canal is distinct. The outer lip is finely ridged inside, and the columella is smooth with a weak parietal nodule. Sculpture of strong granular ridges. A deep depression occurs below the suture. **Colour:** Brown with alternating brown and white spots on ridges, also brown axial streaks. Aperture is white to light brown. **Habitat:** Mainly infratidal down to about 30 m. Extreme low-tide level. **Diet:** Scavenger. **Notes:** The speckled appearance will distinguish this species from *B. cincta*.

Burnupena papyracea
Family Buccinidae (Whelks)

Common
50 mm

Description: A thick shell with a high spire. The whorls are convex and the suture deep. The siphonal canal is short and wide. The outer lip is ridged inside. The columella has a parietal nodule. Sculpture of fine, close spiral threads, sometimes with coarser ridges. Growth-lines are present. **Colour:** Whitish to yellowish brown, aperture is white but sometimes tinged with brown. Periostracum is papery and yellowish brown. **Habitat:** Infratidal, reaching a density of 200 individuals per square metre. Low-tide level. **Diet:** Scavenger. **Notes:** Papery periostracum is characteristic, often encrusted with a purple bryozoan.

Burnupena catarrhacta
Family Buccinidae (Whelks)

Common
48 mm

Description: A shell with a high spire, which is frequently eroded. The aperture has ridges along the inner margin of the outer lip. A blunt nodule occurs in the parietal region. Sculptured by fine spiral striae and growth-lines and a shallow furrow below the suture. **Colour:** Yellowish to dark brown, with dark axial or zigzag flames. Aperture is purplish brown. Columella is marked by a glossy dark brown blotch at the parietal edge. **Habitat:** Shallow pools, in crevices and among mussels in the intertidal zone. **Diet:** Scavenger. **Notes:** In the western Cape these species intergrade with *B. lagenaria*.

Babylonia papillaris
Family Buccinidae (Whelks)

Uncommon
50 mm

Description: A plump shell with a large body whorl. The whorls are convex with narrow rounded shoulders. The suture is fairly deep. The short spire is stepped and the siphonal canal is short and wide. The outer lip is thin and smooth. The columella has a thick callus. The exterior is smooth and shiny. **Colour:** Cream to purplish brown. Covered with reddish-brown spots of differing sizes, which are sometimes axially arranged. **Habitat:** Live shells inhabit infratidal sandy bottoms at depths of 15–65 m. **Diet:** Scavenger. **Notes:** This shell is known as the 'Guinea-fowl' in Jeffreys Bay.

Bullia annulata
Family Nassariidae (Plough Shells)

Common
55 mm

Description: An elongate shell with a high, sharp spire. The whorls are convex with a step-like spiral ridge below the suture. The outer lip is smooth. The columella is not extensive and does not extend up the whorls. Sculptured by weak spiral grooves and fine axial striae. The operculum has smooth edges. **Colour:** Pale buff or yellowish brown, sometimes with a brownish deposit. Purplish spots occur on the subsutural spiral ridge. **Habitat:** Infratidal, occasionally found in sand at low-tide level. **Diet:** Scavenger. **Notes:** The spiral subsutural ridges are absent in KwaZulu-Natal specimens.

Bullia callosa   Common
Family Nassariidae (Plough Shells)   50 mm

Description: A shell with a short, stepped spire and a large body whorl, which gives the shell a deformed appearance. The aperture is fairly large with an extensive parietal callus, which continues up the spire around the suture to form a long sloping cord. A spiral groove is present below the subsutural ridge. **Colour:** Grey-brown to dark brown with a reddish-brown callus. **Habitat:** Infratidal. Empty shells wash up regularly on the beach. **Diet:** Scavenger. **Notes:** *Bullia callosa sulcata* from KwaZulu-Natal is not as heavily callused, and has marked spiral grooves on the body whorl.

Bullia laevissima   Common
Family Nassariidae (Plough Shells)   50 mm

Description: A squat shell with a conical spire. The body whorl and the aperture are large. The smooth callus extends up the suture, practically covering the spire whorls. The exterior is smooth with a shallow subsutural groove on the spire and body whorl. **Colour:** Fawn to brownish grey to fairly dark brown. Columella callus is white, violet or reddish brown. **Habitat:** Mainly infratidal, also half-buried in sand at low-tide level. **Diet:** Scavenger. **Notes:** This species is extremely common in deeper water. The exposed surfaces of the shell are usually badly eroded and covered in algae.

Bullia digitalis

Family Nassariidae (Plough Shells)

Common
52 mm

Description: A narrow shell with a high, tapering spire. The inner lip has a thin shiny callus, which extends as a narrow band above the suture. Shallow grooves occur on the base. Sculptured by fine spiral striae and axial growth-lines. The edges of the operculum are serrated. **Colour:** Light cream to buff and yellow, sometimes with axial brown lines, some violet-brown. Brown line occurs at posterior angle of aperture. **Habitat:** Intertidal. **Diet:** Scavenger. Commonly seen on dead fish, jelly fish and blue bottles. **Notes:** Uses the foot to surf. Leaves distinct wavy tracks on sand in search of carrion.

Bullia diluta

Family Nassariidae (Plough Shells)

Common
30 mm

Description: A narrow shell with a high, tapering spire and convex whorls. The outer lip is rounded and smooth; the columellar callus is thin and just visible above the suture. Sculptured by fine spiral striae. **Colour:** Cream or buff with a row of brown dots below the suture line. Orange-brown axial lines or streaks extend from dots across each whorl. Base is marked with a spiral brown line, a similar line occurs at the posterior end of the aperture. **Habitat:** Mainly infratidal. Common as beach shells. **Diet:** Scavenger. **Notes:** Like all bullias, the animal is blind, but it has a remarkable sense of smell.

Bullia pura

Family Nassariidae (Plough Shells)

Common
34 mm

Description: An elongate shell with a tapering, sharply pointed spire. The outer lip is thin and has fine ridges. The parietal callus is thin with a thick ridge around the base. Sculptured by shallow grooves and flat ridges. **Colour:** Fawn and creamy-orange with faint brown blotches at periphery of last two whorls, and just above suture of spire whorls. **Habitat:** Infratidal, occasionally at low-water level buried in fine sand. **Diet:** Scavenger. **Notes:** Animals brood young under the foot and release them as fully formed juveniles.

Bullia natalensis

Family Nassariidae (Plough Shells)

Common
55 mm

Description: An elongate, straight-sided shell with a high spire and a deep suture. The outer lip is smooth, while the inner lip has a thick callus covering half of each whorl. The exterior is fairly smooth with fine spiral striae, strong short axial ribs below the suture. **Colour:** Fawn to grey-brown with white bands at base and a brown ridge-like line on basal callus. Ribs are light-coloured. Aperture is orange to orange-brown. **Habitat:** Intertidal, in surf where it burrows into sand as the wave retreats. **Diet:** Scavenger. **Notes:** Most abundant plough shell in KwaZulu-Natal and Mozambique.

Bullia mozambicensis   Common
Family Nassariidae (Plough Shells)   34 mm

Description: This shell is similar to *B. natalensis* but smaller. The spire is high and the suture deep. The outer lip is smooth and curved. The callus deposit is not extensive, covering a third of each whorl. Sculptured by shallow spiral grooves and subsutural axial ribs that extend further down the whorl than in *B. natalensis*, giving the surface a granular appearance. **Colour:** Fawn to greyish brown. Aperture is orange-brown. **Habitat:** Intertidal in Mozambique. Infratidal in KwaZulu-Natal. **Diet:** Scavenger. **Notes:** Subsutural axial riblets extend further down whorls of this species than in *B. natalensis*.

Demoulia ventricosa   Common
Family Nassariidae (Mud Snails)   25 mm

Description: A globular, oblong shell with rounded whorls. The pointed apex is often damaged. The outer lip is thick with weak ridge-like teeth, while the inner lip has a heavy callus. The parietal ridge is strong. Sculpture of fine spiral striae. **Colour:** Variable: buff, salmon to light brown flecked with brown; has a necklace of brown and white flecks below the suture. **Habitat:** Mainly infratidal, but may occur in sand at low-tide level. **Diet:** Scavenger. **Notes:** In Jeffreys Bay this shell is called a 'Rosebud'. *D. ventricosa* is replaced in KwaZulu-Natal by *D. v. nataliae*.

Demoulia abbreviata
Family Nassariidae (Mud Snails)

Uncommon
34 mm

Description: A thick, spherical shell with a blunt, conical spire. The whorls are slightly shouldered. The outer lip is thick and ridged inside, while the inner lip has a thick callus shield forming a terminal ridge. Sculpture of low flattened spiral ridges. **Colour:** White, flecked and mottled with brown. The thick, fibrous periostracum is olive-brown. **Habitat:** Mainly infratidal. **Diet:** Scavenger. **Notes:** These shells are known as 'Footballs' in Jeffreys Bay. Shells seldom wash up in a good condition; usually wash up on the beach with a damaged spire.

Nassarius speciosus
Family Nassariidae (Mud Snails)

Common
24 mm

Description: A conical shell with a high, sharp spire. The apex is frequently damaged. The outer lip is thin and weakly ridged inside, while the inner lip has a wide callus extending over half the under side. Sculpture of strong oblique curved axial ribs, which form nodules on the shoulder but become obsolete on the base. **Colour:** Creamy buff to fawn. Beach-worn shells are white with a purple siphonal canal. **Habitat:** Mainly infratidal down to 95 m. **Diet:** Scavenger. **Notes:** Live shell is usually brown, covered by various species of hydroids. Live animals occasionally wash up on beach.

Nassarius glans fenwicki
Family Nassariidae (Mud Snails)

Uncommon
34 mm

Description: A fusiform shell with a high, sharp spire and shouldered whorls. The suture is deep. The outer lip is thin and weakly ridged and the inner lip is smooth. The callus shield is restricted. The exterior is smooth with axial riblets crossed by spiral grooves rendering early whorls granular; obsolete on last two whorls. **Colour:** Yellowish brown. Flecked with white and brown blotches and flames. Spire is violet. **Habitat:** Intertidal, in rock pools. **Diet:** Scavenger. **Notes:** Exposed part covered with algae and is often eroded. These animals live in small colonies buried in sand.

Vasum truncatum
Family Turbinellidae (Vases)

Rare
55 mm

 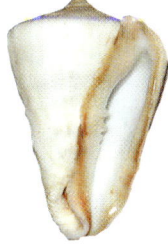

Description: A trigonal, heavy and solid shell. The spire is low and the apex pointed. The angular shoulder has low rounded nodules. The columella is marked with four equal ridges or pleats. Sculptured by unequal spiral cords with weak nodules. **Colour:** Reddish brown to brown, may be off-white. Outer and inner lips are blotched with brown. Aperture is white. **Habitat:** Infratidal. **Diet:** Preys on worms and bivalves. **Notes:** A popular shell with collectors. Best specimens are those that are hauled from fish stomachs, and dived out of the ocean by scuba divers.

Fusinus ocelliferus

Common

Family Fasciolariidae (Horse Conchs)

105 mm

Description: This shell varies considerably in shape, colour, size and sculpture. The spire is high and the apex sharp. The outer lip is ridged inside and the inner lip has a restricted callus. The false umbilicus is deep and the siphonal canal long. Sculpture of strong spiral ridges, one on shoulder is prominent, and often weakly rounded to pointed nodules. **Colour:** Reddish brown to pale buff, often mottled. Operculum is translucent, light yellow. **Habitat:** Below tide level, often buried in sand. **Diet:** Feeds on tube-worms and bivalves. **Notes:** This species has evolved a number of forms (between five and six) along the South African coast.

Fasciolaria lugubris

Common

Family Fasciolariidae (Horse Conchs)

100 mm

Description: A squat shell with a low spire. The protoconch is large, forming a white blunt tip. The outer lip has ridges (sometimes paired) extending into the aperture; the columella has two to three oblique pleats. Sculptured by numerous strong spiral ridges continuing onto the siphonal canal. Whorls have neither a shoulder nor nodules. **Colour:** White to reddish brown. Operculum is dark brown. **Habitat:** Intertidal in sand, between rocks, at low-tide level down to 6 m. **Diet:** Feeds on molluscs and tube-worms. **Notes:** This shell is the only common inshore *Fasciolaria* in the region.

Fasciolaria lugubris heynemanni
Family Fasciolariidae (Horse Conchs)

Uncommon
100 mm

Description: This shell is a subspecies of *F. lugubris*. A fusiform shell with a high spire and shouldered whorls. The protoconch is blunt. The outer lip is smooth inside, while the inner lip has a limited callus glaze. No false umbilicus. Sculpture of well-developed nodules on shoulder and fine spiral striae. **Colour:** Yellowish brown, aperture is white inside. **Habitat:** Infratidal down to about 120 m. **Diet:** Feeds on molluscs and tube-worms. **Notes:** In the Agulhas region, these molluscs occur intertidally in low-tide gulleys and pools, and are squat in shape.

Peristernia forskalii
Family Fasciolariidae (Horse Conchs)

Common
30 mm

Description: A heavy, somewhat squat shell with a high, sharp spire. The outer lip is ridged inside while the inner lip has two to three weak columellar pleats. Sculpture of fairly prominent axial ridges, which reach the suture, and are crossed by fine spiral striae, forming fine spiral subsutural granules. **Colour:** Brown, buff or yellowish on prominent parts of axial ribs. Aperture is brown to purple. **Habitat:** Intertidal on damp exposed rocks, among oysters. **Diet:** Feeds on small worms. **Notes:** A pure white form, *P. forskalii leucothea*, replaces the typical *P. forskalii* south of Durban.

Latirus abnormis
Family Fasciolariidae (Horse Conchs)

Uncommon
70 mm

Description: A fusiform shell with a high spire. The suture is fairly deep, has a deep false umbilicus. The outer lip is smooth with a well-developed notch above the shoulder. The wide siphonal canal has converging sides. Sculpture of fine spiral threads on periphery and base. A fairly deep groove occurs below suture, which is followed by a row of tubercles and a weaker row on body whorl. **Colour:** Orange-brown to light yellow. **Habitat:** Mainly infratidal, at 25–85 m. **Diet:** Feeds on worms and molluscs. **Notes:** Shells in good condition are found only by divers, and hauled from fish stomachs.

Latirus turritus
Family Fasciolariidae (Horse Conchs)

Rare
50 mm

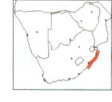

Description: A fairly squat shell with a tapering, high spire and a sharp apex. The siphonal canal is short and oblique. The outer lip is weakly ridged inside and the inner lip has two to three weak columellar pleats. Sculpture of low rounded axial ridges and raised evenly spaced spiral ridges with fine spiral striae in the interspaces. **Colour:** Yellow to light orange, reddish brown on spiral ridges. Aperture is greyish white to yellow. **Habitat:** Mainly infratidal, occasionally found in sand in rock pools at low-tide level. **Diet:** Probably feeds on tube-worms and molluscs. **Notes:** Popular with collectors.

Colubraria obscura
Family Fasciolariidae (Horse Conchs)

Uncommon
55 mm

Description: A solid, elongate shell with a high, tapering spire. The body whorl is large and a rounded varix is present on each whorl. The outer lip is thick with ridge-like teeth. The spiral ridges are crossed by axial ribs, rendering the surface nodular. **Colour:** Cream with brown blotching. Spiral rows of white and brown spots. Brown blotch occurs on varix. Aperture is cream. **Habitat:** Rock dwellers in warmer waters, found intertidally and infratidally where they bury themselves in sand. **Diet:** Probably predatory. **Notes:** This species was formerly classified under the family Collubrariidae.

Amalda contusa
Family Olividae (Olive Shells)

Uncommon
45 mm

Description: A fairly thick shell with a short, tapering spire. The siphonal canal is notched. The inner lip has heavy callus extending up the spire to form a thick blotch of enamel; basal callus is bordered by a spiral furrow. A single oblique groove occurs on the base of the columella. **Colour:** Pinkish brown with a reddish-purple spire enamel, columella and basal callus are purplish brown. **Habitat:** Infratidal. Live specimens come from dredging or from fish stomachs. **Diet:** Scavenger, also preys on live molluscs. **Notes:** Three colour forms occur: yellowish cream, reddish- or purplish brown and pinkish brown.

Amalda obtusa

Family Olividae (Olive Shells)

Common

40 mm

Description: A thick shell with a short spire and a pointed apex. The columella callus extends up the spire. A thick callus pad covers most of the underside of the body whorl. The columellar base has one prominent groove and a few weaker grooves. **Colour:** Greyish brown to light brown over central part of body whorl. Spire enamel is dark glossy brown. White on columella, extends posteriorly to above the suture. **Habitat:** Infratidal in water of about 20–180 m. **Diet:** Scavenger, also preys on molluscs. **Notes:** This shell is easily recognized by the bluntly rounded spire. Usually washes up in worn condition.

Oliva caroliniana

Family Olividae (Olive Shells)

Common

38 mm

Description: A cylindrical shell with a depressed spire. The suture is markedly channelled and the outer lip is thick and smooth. The basal callus has low spiral ridges; callus extends above the anal canal to form a sharp tubercle and a spiral callus ridge. The exterior is smooth and glossy. **Colour:** Fawn to yellowish brown, flecked with reddish-purplish brown. Two dark brown bands occur on body whorl. Aperture is light violet. **Habitat:** Infratidal down to 40 m. **Diet:** Primarily a scavenger, attracted to fish offal. **Notes:** Beach shells in good condition are common.

Oliva tigrina
Family Olividae (Olive Shells)

Rare
50 mm

Description: A heavy shell with a low spire and a pointed apex. The suture is channelled and bordered by a callus ridge, which ends in a small callus pad with a tubercle-like curved ridge at the anal canal. The columella has numerous flat ridges. **Colour:** Creamy-grey, mottled with blue-grey to reddish-brown spots, prominent on outer lip and siphonal notch. Outer lip is dark grey on inside edge. Columella is grey-white. **Habitat:** Infratidal. **Diet:** Scavenger, preys on molluscs. **Notes:** Animal leaves a track in the sand similar to that of moon shells. Beached shells are uncommon, frequently eroded.

Oliva bulbosa
Family Olividae (Olive Shells)

Rare
40 mm

Description: A cylindrical shell, bulbous centrally. The spire is short, with a strong callus ridge bordering the suture. Weak ridges occur on the columella, stronger ridges anteriorly. **Colour:** Variable: cream, spotted blue-grey or with zigzag lines. Spots dark brown on outside of outer lip. Two interrupted brown bands occur on body whorl. Aperture is pale grey with reddish-brown lines on base of columella. **Habitat:** Infratidal, burrowing in sand. **Diet:** Preys on molluscs and small crustaceans, also scavenges. **Notes:** The animal burrows in sand leaving a distinct track.

Oliva tremulina

Family Olividae (Olive Shells)

Rare
85 mm

Description: A cylindrical, heavy shell with a low spire and a sharp apex. The spire suture is channelled. The callus ridge bordering the suture is weak, becoming prominent at the posterior end of the aperture. The inner lip has a narrow callus glaze near the spire, which is wider anteriorly with low rounded spiral ridges. **Colour:** Cream overlaid with reddish-brown spots and zigzag markings. Two broad dark brown transverse bands occur on body whorl. Aperture is white. **Habitat:** Infratidal. **Diet:** Preys on other molluscs. **Notes:** A species that is sought after by collectors. Beach shells are usually worn.

Melapium lineatum

Family Melapiidae (Onion Shells)

Uncommon
30 mm

Description: A bulbous shell with a low, blunt spire and a large aperture. The body whorl is roundly shouldered. The outer lip is strongly curved; the inner lip with a thick callus forms a large rounded parietal thickening. The columella is concave. Sculptured by coarse growth-lines and a sharp basal ridge. **Colour:** White to cream with straight, wavy or interrupted brown to reddish-brown axial lines and dark brown peripheral blotches. **Habitat:** Infratidal in 30–160 m of water. **Diet:** Preys on molluscs, also scavenges. **Notes:** Known as 'Onion Shells'. Shells in good condition occasionally wash up.

Callipara bullatiana
Family Volutidae (Volutes)

Uncommon
65 mm

Description: An elongate, oval shell with a low, blunt spire. A blunt protoconch is present in adults. The aperture is long and narrow. The outer lip extends up the spire; has two columella pleats. The exterior is smooth; sculptured by weak growth-lines. **Colour:** Light brown to flesh-colour with dark brown flecks. Paired dark brown lines occur behind outer lip, spots on outer edge. Columella is creamy-orange. May have chocolate-brown spot at posterior end of outer lip. **Habitat:** Infratidal in sand pockets. Active burrowers. **Diet:** Primarily predatory, also scavenges. **Notes:** Known as 'Moles' or 'Dachshund' in Jeffreys Bay.

Harpa amouretta
Family Harpidae (Harps)

Rare
50 mm

Description: An oblong shell with a short, stepped spire and a sharp apex. The aperture is narrower in comparison with other species. The inner lip is smooth with a thin callus glaze. 11–12 strong flat ribs occur on each whorl. The shoulder is angular. The posterior ends of the ribs are pointed, followed by a second row of sharp, weaker spines. **Colour:** Brown to reddish brown with zigzag axial lines and creamy-white to dark brown spiral bands. Ventral zone has two to three brown blotches. **Habitat:** Infratidal in sand to 2–10 m. **Diet:** Preys on molluscs, crustaceans, also scavenges. **Notes:** An attractive, popular shell.

Harpa major
Family Harpidae (Harps)

Rare
90 mm

Description: A shell with a depressed spire and a sharp apex. The aperture is wide. The shell surface is covered with strong, broad, curved axial ribs. Sharp nodules occur on the posterior ends of the ribs. **Colour:** Light brown to pink with vivid pink or reddish-brown wavy axial marks. Lighter and darker spiral bands occur on body whorl. Dark brown to nearly black posterior and mid-body blotches divided by a pale central marking. **Habitat:** Infratidal down to 200–275 m. **Diet:** Preys on other molluscs and crustaceans. **Notes:** The name 'Harpa' is derived from the strong axial ribs reminiscent of the strings of a harp.

Marginella ornata
Family Marginellidae (Margin Shells)

Common
28 mm

Description: A squat shell with a short spire and convex whorls. The outer lip is thick and the edge smooth. The columella has four pleats. The exterior is smooth. **Colour:** Ranges from grey, light brown, yellowish brown to wine-red; has pale spiral bands or lines with grey or brown flecks or dots. Back of outer lip is brown to reddish brown with almost black flecks. **Habitat:** Infratidal. **Diet:** Preys on small gastropods and bivalves. **Notes:** Specimens in good condition are rare and therefore shells collected live by divers are expensive to purchase.

Marginella mosaica
Family Marginellidae (Margin Shells)

Uncommon
32 mm

Description: A medium-sized shell with a short spire and a fairly wide aperture. The outer lip is thick, the edge is smooth. The columella has four strong pleats. The exterior is smooth with fine growth-lines and the shoulder is strong. **Colour:** White or buff with spiral rows of dark grey or brown rod-like spots, sometimes with diffuse axial waves of greyish-brown colour, edged with dark brown. **Habitat:** Infratidal in sand. **Diet:** Preys on gastropods and bivalves, but also feeds on carrion. **Notes:** This uncommon and attractive shell is a sought-after collector's item.

Marginella rosea
Family Marginellidae (Margin Shells)

Common
25 mm

Description: The shell has four columellar pleats. The spire is high with convex whorls and the shoulder is weak. The exterior is smooth and glossy. The thick outer lip has a notch anterior to the anal notch. **Colour:** Colour is determined by locality. Ground colour is pink, yellowish, grey-white with white flecks. Wavy bands are edged with dark lines or fine brown axial lines. Outer lip has dark brown, grey spots or short bars. **Habitat:** Intertidal on sand and rocks, also infratidally down to 50 m. **Diet:** Preys on gastropods, bivalves; eats carrion. **Notes:** Only species with a distinctive notch on outer lip.

Marginella lussii

Family Marginellidae (Margin Shells)

Rare
26 mm

Description: This shell is similar in shape to *M. ornata*. The spire is short and the whorls convex. The shoulder is slightly less rounded. The columella has four strong pleats and the outer surface is smooth. **Colour:** Pink with brown wavy axial or zigzag lines. Reddish-brown flecks cover the outer edge of the outer lip. The base of the columella is white. **Habitat:** Infratidal in sand. **Diet:** Preys on molluscs, also eats carrion. **Notes:** Specimens wash up on the beach but are seldom in good condition. Live specimens with attractive colour patterns are collected by divers in deeper water.

Mitra picta

Family Mitridae (Mitres)

Common
38 mm

Description: An oval, fusiform shell with a high spire. The siphonal canal is short and broad and the outer lip has weak teeth. The columella has three to five pleats. Sculptured by pitted spiral grooves that become prominent on the base. **Colour:** Light to dark brown with irregular white streaks and white blotches. Aperture is brown to greyish brown. **Habitat:** Infratidal. Beach shells are common. **Diet:** Predatory, paralyses prey, such as worms and gastropods, with toxic saliva. **Notes:** Shells are called 'Dates' in Jeffreys Bay. Another subspecies, occurring further west, is called *M. picta aerumnosa*.

Mitra latruncularia
Family Mitridae (Mitres)

Common
28 mm

Description: This shell is similar to *M. picta* but smaller and less fusiform. Sculptured by prominent spiral grooves with rounded intervals between the grooves. Extremely small axial threads cross the spiral grooves, resulting in a finely punctured appearance. **Colour:** Light to dark brown, flecked with white, and specks of brown and orange, particularly on a pale band below the suture. **Habitat:** Mainly infratidal, occasionally found in sand in low-tide pools under loose stones. **Diet:** Preys on worms and gastropods. **Notes:** *M. l albozonata* replaces *M. latruncularia* east of Port Alfred.

Mitra limbifera
Family Mitridae (Mitres)

Common
36 mm

Description: A fusiform shell with a high spire. The inner lip has four to five pleats and the columella shield is raised at the edge. Sculptured by shallow spiral grooves separated by low rounded ridges, base has well-developed grooves. **Colour:** Spire and posterior part of body whorl is white, rest of body whorl is brown. A thin brown line may be present above the spire suture. Aperture is greyish white to brown. **Habitat:** In low-tide pools in sand, under stones. Infratidal down to 2 m. **Diet:** Preys on worms and gastropods. **Notes:** Shells occupied by hermit crabs are often found in rock pools.

Mitra litterata
Family Mitridae (Mitres)

Common

25 mm

Description: A squat shell with a short spire that ends in a sharp point. Siphonal canal is short, very broad and notched. The smooth outer lip is strong, with a central thickening. The columella has four to five strong pleats. Sculptured by spiral rows of pits, which become less conspicuous on later whorls. **Colour:** White with irregular broken wavy dark brown axial bands. Periostracum is translucent yellow. **Habitat:** Intertidal in marine growth, under rocks. **Diet:** Feeds on worms which are swallowed whole. **Notes:** Animals are frequently seen between polyps of the soft coral *Palythoa nelliae*.

Mitra punctostriata
Family Mitridae (Mitres)

Uncommon

35 mm

Description: A fusiform shell with a high, sharp spire. The outer lip is thin; the inner lip has four to five strong columellar pleats. The exterior sculptured with shallow grooves with very fine holes, which are obsolete on the body whorl. The base has more prominent spiral grooves. **Colour:** Yellow to brown with white axial streaks and a subsutural necklace of alternating white and brown spots and flecks. **Habitat:** Infratidal among rocks. **Diet:** Preys on worms. **Notes:** Shells in fairly good condition can sometimes be collected on the beach.

Trigonostoma foveolata
Family Cancellariidae (Nutmeg Shells)

Common
22 mm

Description: An oval, fusiform shell with stepped whorls and a triangular aperture. The shoulder is keeled and its slope concave. The outer lip is curved and raised posteriorly. The columella has three folds. Low rounded axial ribs occur on the body whorl. Sculpture of weak spiral threads. **Colour:** Cream, light brown to dark brown or violet, occasionally blotched with brown or with brown axial lines. **Habitat:** Infratidal. Occasionally in low-tide pools in sand among rocks. **Diet:** Animals draw minute particles into their mouths but little is known about their biology. **Notes:** Known as 'Steps' in Jeffreys Bay.

Trigonostoma semidisjuncta
Family Cancellariidae (Nutmeg Shells)

Common
22 mm

Description: A squat shell with a low spire, stepped whorls and a triangular aperture. The shoulder is keeled and the suture is deep and widely channelled. The umbilicus is large and deep. The last part of the body whorl is attached to or slightly separated from the ultimate whorl. Sculptured by spiral striae and low axial ribs. Strong ribs occur, sometimes in the channelled suture. **Colour:** Cream to fawn with reddish-brown mottling and axial lines. **Habitat:** Infratidal. Beach shells are common. **Diet:** Minute planktonic particles. **Notes:** Known as 'Basket Steps' in Jeffreys Bay.

Clionella sinuata
Family Turridae (Turrids)

Common
45 mm

Description: An elongate shell with a high, straight spire. The apex is usually eroded. The anal sinus is shallow and situated on a raised cord. The exterior is sculptured by coarse or weak axial ribs that turn oblique below the suture. A depression is present below the suture. **Colour:** Light brown to grey. Periostracum is black to dark brown. **Habitat:** Intertidal in low-tide pools under loose rocks, usually half buried in muddy sand. **Diet:** Probably scavenger. **Notes:** The exposed part of the shell and the spire is often eroded.

Clionella bornii
Family Turridae (Turrids)

Common
38 mm

Description: This species is smaller and narrower than *C. sinuata*. The spire is long, tapering and straight. The anal sinus is shallow. The subsutural cord is followed by a shallow depression. Sculpture of fairly strong oblique axial ridges. **Colour:** The shell is white or buff with a thin olive-brown periostracum. **Habitat:** Intertidal zone under stones and in sand. **Diet:** Scavenger. **Notes:** Formerly considered as a subspecies of *C. sinuata*, but recently accepted to be a full species.

Clionella krausii
Family Turridae (Turrids)

Common
35 mm

Description: An elongate shell with a high spire. The whorls have a wide subsutural depression above the shoulder. The short axial ribs form distinct nodules at the shoulder. The spiral striae are fine. The anal sinus is situated in a depression instead of in a raised cord. **Colour:** White, marked with brown. Axial ridges are lighter in colour than the interspaces. Periostracum is brown. **Habitat:** In pools at low spring-tide level under loose rocks. In estuaries. **Diet:** Scavenger. **Notes:** A small form occurs in the False Bay – Cape Agulhas area.

Clionella tripartita
Family Turridae (Turrids)

Common
45 mm

Description: The spire is high, tapering, and straight. The axial ribs are oblique, short and preceded by a smooth band and a nodular sutural cord. The anal sinus is deep and L-shaped. Fine spiral striae mark the surface, becoming granular on the base. **Colour:** Buff or pale grey with white and brown markings. Sutural cord has alternating white and brown spots. Surface is shiny. **Habitat:** Infratidal. Beach shells are common and may be found in low-tide pools under rocks and in sand. **Diet:** Scavenger. **Notes:** The anal sinus differentiates this species from other members of this genus.

Clionella rosaria
Family Turridae (Turrids)

Common
24 mm

Description: The shell is identified by its sharp, tapering and straight spire. The sutural cord is narrow and bead-like. The subsutural depression is shallow with an L-shaped anal sinus at the suture. The axial ribs are narrow and the spiral striae fine. **Colour:** Pink or orange, sometimes mottled with white. Sutural cord is white with brown spots. The periostracum is absent. **Habitat:** Intertidal in low-tide pools under rocks, among coralline algae on submerged rocks. **Diet:** Scavenger, probably also feeds on small marine organisms. **Notes:** The sutural cord is white in *C. r. kowiensis*.

Conus betulinus
Family Conidae (Cones)

Uncommon
90 mm

Description: A heavy, pyriform shell. The spire is low with a projecting apex. The shoulder is strongly rounded and smooth without spiral sculpture but has axial growth-lines. The exterior is smooth with spiral grooves on the base. **Colour:** Yellowish brown to orange with spiral rows of blackish dots, larger on the spire and shoulder slope. Dark brown periostracum is thick and fibrous. **Habitat:** Mainly infratidal, may be found intertidally in pools under sand. **Diet:** Probably feeds on polychaete worms and other molluscs. **Notes:** This species was common in Durban bay once, but it is rarely found now.

Conus biliosus
Family Conidae (Cones)

Common
50 mm

Description: A conical shell with slightly convex sides. The shoulder is somewhat rounded, sometimes with weak nodules. The spire is low and straight. Sculpture of weak spiral striae, which are stronger on the base. **Colour:** Grey to olive-brown, spiral rows of brown spots and dark brown axial steaks. Pale on shoulder and middle of body whorl. Fibrous periostracum is yellowish brown. **Habitat:** Infratidal, and rock pools with sandy bottoms, crevices and caverns at low-tide level. **Diet:** Feeds on worms. **Notes:** The South African species is referred to as *C. b. meyeri* by certain authors.

Conus catus
Family Conidae (Cones)

Uncommon
35 mm

Description: A thick, heavy shell with a low spire and a rounded shoulder. The spiral lirae on the body whorl become stronger and ridge-like on the base. Sculptured by axial growth-lines. **Colour:** Two colour forms identified: bluish white mottled with dark bluish-black colours, or bluish white with brown blotches. Aperture is pale grey. Edge of lip is reddish brown. Lilac to pink apex. **Habitat:** On sand in rock pools at low-tide level. **Diet:** Feeds mostly on polychaete worms. **Notes:** Some authors believe this to be a poisonous, fish-eating species.

Conus chaldeus
Family Conidae (Cones)

Common
30 mm

Description: The spire of this shell is raised, the shoulder rounded and nodular. The spiral grooves on the spire become more prominent on the body whorl. **Colour:** White flecks occur on spire and shoulder. Body whorl has axial stripes with black and purplish markings. Pinkish-white median band is transected by black axial stripes. Aperture is bluish white; edge of lip is black. **Habitat:** Rock pools, or in rock crevices and gulleys. May be found on exposed rocks in the intertidal zone. **Diet:** Feeds on polychaete worms. **Notes:** This species is widely distributed throughout Indo-Pacific Ocean.

Conus ebraeus
Family Conidae (Cones)

Common
40 mm

Description: This shell is similar to *C. chaldeus* but bigger. The spire is low and eroded, the sides convex and the shoulder rounded and nodular. Weak spiral threads occur on the base. **Colour:** Pinkish white banded with three rows of irregular black, rectangular blotches on the body whorl. Spire and base are similarly marked. Aperture is bluish white. Black blotches occur on lip. **Habitat:** Rock pools, in rock crevices, in gulleys and often on exposed rocks. **Diet:** Feeds on polychaete worms. **Notes:** This species has the same extensive distribution range as *C. chaldeus*.

Conus lividus
Family Conidae (Cones)

Common
42 mm

Description: This shell has a low spire with fine spiral lines; the apex is usually worn. The shoulder is angular with nodules. The body whorl has fine spiral lines that become increasingly coarse and granular on the base. **Colour:** Olive-brown, base is darker. Shoulder and spire are white. Pale median band. Aperture is violet. Pale median zone shines through. Outer edge of lip is yellow. **Habitat:** Low-tide pools, in sand, under stones or in muddy crevices. **Diet:** Feeds on polychaete and other worms. **Notes:** The nodules on the shoulder of the shell distinguish this species from *C. flavidus*.

Conus flavidus
Family Conidae (Cones)

Common
40 mm

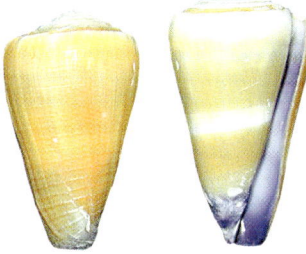

Description: A fairly heavy shell with straight sides. The spire is depressed, the shoulder rounded and smooth (compare with *C. lividus*, which has nodules on the shoulder). The early whorls are usually eroded. Sculpture of granular spiral ridges crossed by growth-lines. **Colour:** Orange to olive-brown, white band on shoulder and mid-body whorl. Aperture is violet with a white median zone. **Habitat:** Rock pools with sandy bottoms in the intertidal zone. **Diet:** Feeds mainly on polychaete worms. **Notes:** The species *C. sanguinolenus* does not have a median white band.

Conus miles
Family Conidae (Cones)

Common
60 mm

Description: A heavy shell with convex sides. The spire is short and the apex blunt. The shoulder is rounded and angular. Sculpture of growth-lines and widely spaced spiral threads on the base. **Colour:** Base and median zone are dark brown. Numerous fine brown axial lines occur on spire and body whorl. The aperture is white and dark brown, corresponding to brown exterior. **Habitat:** Mainly infratidal; may be found in low-tide pools in sand and under stones. **Diet:** Feeds on polychaete worms. **Notes:** Although not common in South Africa, this species is common in Mozambique and further north.

Conus natalis
Family Conidae (Cones)

Common
45 mm

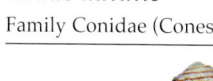

Description: A shell with a depressed spire. The angular shoulder is smoothly rounded and the shoulder slope is concave and axially ridged. The base of the body whorl is markedly ridged. **Colour:** White or pale violet. Triangular markings are arranged in bands, broken transverse bands or in some, only two transverse bands of broken patches. Spire and shoulder slope are brown with white blotches. **Habitat:** Muddy and sandy pools at and below the low-water level. **Diet:** Preys on gastropods, particularly *Diloma* species (*see* pp 21–23). **Notes:** More common in the southern Transkei than in KwaZulu-Natal.

Conus rattus
Family Conidae (Cones)

Uncommon
35 mm

Description: A shell with slightly convex sides. The spire is depressed and the apex sharp. The shoulder is angular and the concave shoulder slope has weak spiral threads. Sculptured by weak spiral grooves on the body whorl, which become stronger on the base. **Colour:** Dark brown. White blotches occur on shoulder. Rows of white dots and small blotches mark the body whorl. Aperture is purple. **Habitat:** Low-tide pools down to 5 m. Usually half buried in sand near or under rocks. **Diet:** Preys on polychaete worms. **Notes:** The white blotches on the shoulder are a diagnostic feature in this species.

Conus tinianus
Family Conidae (Cones)

Common
50 mm

Description: A light, thin shell with a low spire, prominent suture and convex sides. Fine spiral striae occur on the flattened shoulder slope and base. **Colour:** Extremely variable: uniform orange, pink or violet. Ground colour is violet or white flecked and blotched with brown to reddish brown, sometimes spiral lines of dots and dashes. **Habitat:** Infratidal. In rock pools under stones. **Diet:** Feeds on polychaete worms and probably gastropods. **Notes:** This species is the most common of the southern African cones, adorned with the most variable colour patterns.

Hydatina amplustre
Family Hydatinidae (Bubble Shells)

Uncommon
20 mm

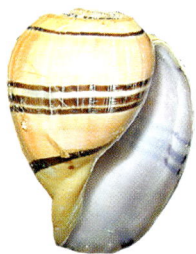

Description: A small, fragile and almost pear-shaped shell with a depressed but exposed spire and a channelled suture. The aperture is narrow and the exterior is very smooth and glossy. **Colour:** White with two broad transverse pink bands bordered by thin black lines. The central white band is occasionally replaced by a black band. **Habitat:** Mainly infratidal. During the summer months, animals are found in muddy sand among rocks in protected pools. **Diet:** Feeds on polychaete worms. **Notes:** The shell does not fully contain the very colourful animal.

Hydatina physis
Family Hydatinidae (Bubble Shells)

Uncommon
35 mm

Description: A thin, fragile shell that may be globular or oval. The aperture is wide and the spire depressed or sunken. The umbilicus is slit-like. The exterior is smooth and covered with numerous fine growth-lines. **Colour:** Cream with numerous thin black, or brown, slightly wavy spiral lines. Periostracum is yellowish. **Habitat:** Sand flats or in rock pools. **Diet:** Feeds exclusively on burrowing polychaete worms. **Notes:** Most abundant in summer. The animals form small colonies. *H. physis* occurs in sheltered waters, whereas *H. p. vesicaria* occurs on the open coast.

Hydatina zonata
Family Hydatinidae (Bubble Shells)

Rare
28 mm

Description: A thin, fragile and globular shell with a flattened spire and a channelled suture. The aperture is large and the umbilicus is absent. The exterior is smooth and glossy. **Colour:** Cream with three cream spiral bands: below the suture, at the base and at the middle of body whorl, demarcated by four blackish-brown spiral lines. Two zones of numerous fine brown axial lines occur on body whorl. **Habitat:** Low-tide banks of muddy sand in lagoons and estuaries. **Diet:** Feeds on polychaete worms. **Notes:** Like the other bubble shells, the live animal itself is more attractive than the shell.

Bulla ampulla
Family Bullidae (Flask Bubbles)

Common
45 mm

Description: A thin shell that may be globular or oval. The spire is sunken and the exterior smooth. The outer lip is thin, raised posteriorly and evenly curved. The thickened lower part is continuous with the columella. **Colour:** Creamy white, mottled with various shades of brown. **Habitat:** Muddy sand in estuaries, among eelgrass and in sandy gulleys. **Diet:** Herbivorous, feeds on small seaweeds. **Notes:** Each living shell is enclosed in a cocoon of mucus and sand grains. Specimens from the colder southern part of their range are smaller than those from the warmer northern part of the range.

Akera soluta
Family Akeridae

Uncommon
40 mm

Description: A thin, fragile and cylindrical shell with a depressed spire. The suture is widely channelled. The outer lip is evenly curved; the columella plate is very thin. The exterior is smooth and glossy. Sculptured by fine spiral striae and axial growth-lines. Periostracum is thin and smooth. **Colour:** Yellowish, creamy and translucent. **Habitat:** Shallow grass beds, in sheltered pools and in tidal swimming pools. **Diet:** Herbivorous, feeds on algae. **Notes:** The animal burrows into the sand. Only the siphon protrudes from the surface of the sand.

Umbraculum umbraculum
Family Umbraculidae (Umbrella shells)

Uncommon
50 mm

Description: A flattened shell that is more or less elliptical. The apex is depressed and slightly off-centre. The exterior has numerous growth-lines and weak axial rays. The internal surface is smooth. **Colour:** Colour is yellowish white with a brown central blotch and a bluish apex. **Habitat:** Mainly in low-tide pools and gulleys among rocks. Only the shells wash up on the beach. **Diet:** Feeds on sponges and algae. **Notes:** The body of the animal is much larger than the shell, which is attached to the top side of the animal.

Siphonaria capensis
Family Siphonariidae (False Limpets)

Common
25 mm

Description: An oblong, oval or angular shell that is compressed, yet fairly high. A raised area accommodates the siphon that extends from the lung cavity. The apex is usually eroded. Sculptured by numerous flattened radial ribs. **Colour:** Ribs are grey, intervals are greyish brown with brown radial lines. Centre of internal surface is orange brown to dark brown or milky. **Habitat:** Rock pools and on exposed flat rocks in mid-tidal zone. Returns to home-scar after feeding. **Diet:** Feeds on algae and lichen. **Notes:** These animals can tolerate sand-cover. They leave thin sand-tracks on rocks.

Siphonaria oculus
Family Siphonariidae (False Limpets)

Common
25 mm

Description: This shell is similar to *S. capensis*. The apex is not always eroded. Numerous radial ribs of various thicknesses project at the margin, rendering it crenulate. **Colour:** Ribs are grey, intervals are brownish grey. Interior is glossy and dark brown with radiating pale brown lines around edge, and a central transverse white blotch. **Habitat:** Sheltered rocks in lagoons and estuaries. On walls in tidal pools and wharfs. **Diet:** Grazes on algae, returning to a distinct home-scar. **Notes:** The white interior blotch differentiates this shell from *S. capensis*.

Siphonaria concinna
Family Siphonariidae (False Limpets)

Common
25 mm

Description: An oblong shell of medium height with a worn apex. Unequal axial ribs project at the margin. **Colour:** Ribs are pale grey, intervals are brownish grey. Interior is dark brown to black with radiating white lines, and has a large central white deposit. **Habitat:** Lives in groups on exposed rocks, forming home-scars. **Diet:** Feeds on black lichens and encrusting algae. **Notes:** Juveniles have iridescent blue-green flecks on the shell surface, and are called *S. c.* fm. *cyaneomaculata*. In *S. c.* fm. *albofasciata*, the ribs are fused into fewer, strong flat ribs.

Callochiton dentatus
Family Ischnochitonidae (Chitons)

Common
45 mm

Description: A depressed, broad and oblong shell. The girdle is leathery, soft and smooth and the valves are wide and flat. The lateral areas are slightly raised. The surface appears finely granular. The insertion plates have four slits. **Colour:** Brown, mottled with orange, yellow, green and pink. Interior is purplish pink. **Habitat:** Infratidal; and under loose rocks in low-tide pools. **Diet:** Grazer, rasping encrusting algae or small animals from the rocks at night. **Notes:** The animal is easily recognized by its smooth shell and leathery girdle.

Chaetopleura papilio
Family Ischnochitonidae (Chitons)

Uncommon
60 mm

Description: A fairly large shell with a wide girdle that is covered with stiff erect bristles. The valves are arched with a weak median ridge. The lateral areas are only slightly raised. The median area is longitudinally striate, lateral areas and end valves have growth-lines. Insertion plate has only one slit. **Colour:** Dark brown, polished surface. Interior is yellowish brown. Girdle is dark brown. **Habitat:** Under loose rocks in low-tide pools. **Diet:** Feeds on algae scraped off the rocks with the coarse radula. **Notes:** The shell is shiny and smooth, resembling a piece of polished wood.

Chaetopleura pertusa
Family Ischnochitonidae (Chitons)

Uncommon
40 mm

Description: An oblong shell. The girdle is covered with sparse bristles, some short, others longer and branched. The granular threads are longitudinal on the median area, radial on raised lateral areas and end valves. A single slit occurs on the intermediate valves. **Colour:** Variable, with orange, red, pink, yellow or brown mottling. **Habitat:** Under rocks in low-tide pools. **Diet:** Mainly herbivorous. In its effort to scrape algae off the rocks, it also ingests other marine animals. **Notes:** Some of these animals exhibit the brightest and loveliest colours of all the southern African chitons.

Dinoplax gigas
Family Ischnochitonidae (Chitons)

Common
100 mm

Description: The largest southern African chiton has a narrow girdle with tufts of small spines. The valves are high and arched. The median area is distinct, the lateral areas are raised. The lateral areas and end valves have radial riblets. The median area is finely pitted. **Colour:** Valves brown, mottled in young animals. Grey and eroded in older animals. **Habitat:** Intertidal pools under rocks, often covered with sand. **Diet:** Mainly herbivorous. **Notes:** These chitons are known as 'Armadillos' among anglers, who use them as bait. Collection of this species is controlled by legislation.

Dinoplax fossus
Family Ischnochitonidae (Chitons)

Common
80 mm

Description: A large shell with a fairly narrow girdle that is covered with short glassy spindles. The valves are steeply arched. The shell has a distinct median angle. The lateral areas are raised with strong radial ribs, while the median areas and end valves have slash-like pits. **Colour:** Brown, speckled with bluish-grey and pale areas. Beaks of valves in juveniles are orange. Valves are often eroded in older animals. **Habitat:** Low-tide pools, under loose rocks. **Diet:** Scrapes algae off the rocks at night. **Notes:** *Odostomia chitonicola*, a small gastropod, lives as a parasite among the girdle spines of this chiton.

Dinoplax validifossus
Family Ischnochitonidae (Chitons)

Common
80 mm

Description: A large shell, similar to *D. fossus*. The girdle is narrow and evenly covered with glassy spindles. The valves are high; the lateral areas raised and radially ridged. The median area has distinct radial longitudinal threads rendering the surface coarse or fibrous. **Colour:** Dark brown, speckled with paler spots. **Habitat:** Low-tide pools under loose stones. **Diet:** Grazes on algae-covered rocks at night. **Notes:** A tiny bivalve, *Montacuta natalensis*, lives on the underside of the foot and girdle of this species, possibly also in *D. fossus*.

Chiton tulipa
Family Chitonidae (Chitons)

Common
45 mm

Description: A medium-sized, oval shell. The girdle is thick, fairly wide, covered with smooth scales. The valves are steeply arched and beaked. The lateral areas prominent and smooth. Intermediate plates have one slit. **Colour:** Variable, flecked with various colours. Interior is pale blue-green. Girdle with a few bars of dark brown. A brightly coloured chiton. **Habitat:** Low-tide pools on the underside of loose rocks. **Diet:** Scrapes algae off the rocks. **Notes:** This is one of the most attractive chitons in the region.

Onithochiton literatus
Family Chitonidae (Chitons)

Common
50 mm

Description: A long shell with parallel sides. The middle is relatively narrow; the girdle is broad and smooth. The valves are arched and the beak flattened. The shell has slightly raised lateral areas. The head and tail valves have radial ribs, which break into small nodules. Eyes present on radially ribbed areas. Adults are badly eroded. **Colour:** Girdle is brown with paler marks. Immature and protected shells are buff with orange-brown flecks. **Habitat:** Rocks exposed to heavy wave-action resulting in severe erosion. **Diet:** Feeds on algae and probably small marine animals. **Notes:** The habitat is unique to this species.

Achanthochitona garnoti
Family Acanthochitonidae (Chitons)

Common
40 mm

Description: A depressed, broadly oval shell with a wide girdle that is covered with fine spicules and 18 tufts of radiating glassy spicules. Sculptured by fine elongate granules. The jugal tract has longitudinal striae. The valves are eroded in adults. **Colour:** Dark brown to black with two diverging white stripes lateral to jugal tract. Interior is bluish green; central purple-brown spot. **Habitat:** Exposed rocks and crevices in the mid-tidal zone. **Diet:** Grazes on algae. **Notes:** The glassy spicules of this chiton can cause severe irritation to the skin.

Argonauta argo

Uncommon
150 mm

Family Argonautidae (Nautilus Shells)

Description: A thin, brittle shell that is large and flat. Two keels are present around the edge, and are studded with low conical knobs. The aperture is large, and widest adjacent to the curved apex. Each ridge on the sides ends with a tubercle. **Colour:** Glossy white. **Habitat:** Floats near the surface of the sea. **Diet:** Preys on pelagic molluscs and other planktonic animals. **Notes:** Only females produce shells, which are secreted by the first pair of arms. The shell serves as a protective housing for the female and her eggs. The male is small and has no shell.

Spirula spirula

Common
20 mm

Family Spirulidae (Spirulas)

Description: A small, fragile shell that is loosely coiled. The shell is divided internally by partitions to form chambers linked by a central tube. **Colour:** The gas-filled tube is white. **Habitat:** Lives offshore in water of 100–1200 m. The gas-filled horns wash up on beaches worldwide. **Diet:** Carnivorous. **Notes:** The live animal hangs head-down and varies the gas and liquid contents of the chambers of the shell in order to control its buoyancy.

Sepia officinalis vermiculata
Family Sepiidae (Cuttlefish)

Common
150 mm

Description: A broad shell, tapering at the anterior and posterior ends. The dorsal surface is covered by tubercles and the dorsal ridge is absent. A small sharp-pointed spine occurs posteriorly. The shell has a median longitudinal ridge. A ventral zone of striations extends over half the length of the shell. **Colour:** The cuttlebone, or internal shell, is white. **Habitat:** Shallow water to great depths. **Diet:** Preys on crustaceans and molluscs. **Notes:** This cuttlebone belongs to the largest of the southern African cuttlefish. The gas fluid content in the cuttlebone can be modified to regulate buoyancy.

Dentalium regulare
Family Dentaliidae (Tusk Shells)

Common
30 mm

Description: A tube-like, evenly curved shell. A shallow terminal notch occurs at the apex. Sculpture of strong, widely spaced longitudinal ribs. With growth, the weaker intermediate ribs develop in intervals, which are separated by shallow grooves. **Colour:** White when fresh, pink or orange when beach-worn. **Habitat:** Infratidal sandy bottoms. **Diet:** Feeds on single-celled algae, worms and organic debris. **Notes:** Animals are usually partly or wholly buried in sand with the narrow end projecting from the surface. Shells commonly wash up on the beach, mostly in a worn condition.

Glycymeris queketti
Family Glycymeridae (Bittersweet Clams)

Uncommon
65 mm

Description: A heavy, ear-shaped shell with rounded ends. Sculptured by flattened ribs radiating from the prominent umbo. The interior margin has ridge-like teeth. The periostracum is thick, fibrous and brown. **Colour:** Exterior of shell is yellowish to reddish brown. Interior is white with muscle scars tinged with brown. **Habitat:** Infratidal down to 20–100 m. **Diet:** Strain microscopic plants and animals out of the water. **Notes:** The single valves of these shells often wash up in a worn state on KwaZulu-Natal beaches.

Glycymeris connollyi
Family Glycymeridae (Bittersweet Clams)

Common
18 mm

Description: An ear-shaped or slightly trigonal shell with a prominent umbo. The exterior is sculptured by narrow, rounded radial threads; the interior margin is crenulate. The thin periostracum is light brown. **Colour:** White, blotched with brown or concentric brown markings or bands. Interior is white to reddish brown, especially near the umbo. **Habitat:** Lives in sand in 20–100 m of water. **Diet:** Strains food particles from surrounding water. **Notes:** Single valves are commonly washed up on sandy beaches, but are usually in worn condition.

Arca avellana
Family Arcidae (Ark Shells)

Common
35 mm

Description: An oblong, fairly heavy shell with a straight dorsal margin. An angular ridge extends from the umbo to the posterior end. The byssal gape is wide. The exterior has fine radial threads and growth-lines. **Colour:** Off-white, interior stained with purple-brown. The periostracum is yellowish brown and bristle-like. **Habitat:** Attached via byssus threads to underside of rocks. **Diet:** Filters food particles from the water. **Notes:** Specimens frequently wash up on the beach with both valves intact. Malformed species are common.

Barbatia foliata
Family Arcidae (Ark Shells)

Common
70 mm

Description: A rectangular shell with a wide byssal gape, often resulting in an indentation of the ventral margin. Sculptured by numerous radial riblets, which are crossed by concentric growth-lines rendering the sculpture granular in fresh shells. **Colour:** White, covered by a bristly blackish-brown periostracum. **Habitat:** Low-tide pools attached by byssus threads to the underside of loose rocks. **Diet:** Filters suspended food particles from the water. **Notes:** These shells wash up regularly on the beach, often with both valves intact.

Barbatia obliquata
Family Arcidae (Ark Shells)

Common
58 mm

Description: A shell with elongate valves, which are markedly higher posteriorly than anteriorly, giving the shell an oblique appearance. The ventral margin is concave. Sculptured by fine radial threads, which are crossed by concentric growth-lines. The periostracum is dark brown, bristly and often worn. **Colour:** White, the umbonal and posterior area are tinged with brown. **Habitat:** Attached by byssus threads to underside of rocks in sandy pools at low-tide level. **Diet:** Filters food particles from water. **Notes:** Shells with both valves intact commonly wash up on the beach.

Aulacomya ater
Family Mytilidae (Mussels)

Common
60 mm

Description: An elongate, wedge-shaped shell with a sharp, curved umbo situated at the anterior end of the valve. Sculptured by coarse, wavy radial ribs. The black periostracum is pliable. **Colour:** Exterior is violet; umbonal area is eroded up to nacreous layer. Interior is white with purple streaks. **Habitat:** The Ribbed Mussel inhabits the cold water of the western Cape, forming dense colonies on intertidal rocks, where they are pounded by waves. **Diet:** Filters food particles from water. **Notes:** This species is also found in New Zealand and South America.

Choromytilus meridionalis
Family Mytilidae (Mussels)

Common
120 mm

Description: An elongate shell with a terminal umbo. The exterior is smooth with concentric growth-lines. **Colour:** Surface is violet-black while the interior is milky or bluish white. The pliable periostracum is ink-black and flakes when the shell is dried out. **Habitat:** The Black Mussel occurs abundantly in the cold water of the Cape on exposed rocks and shallow reefs in the lower mid-tidal region, particularly in areas subject to sand cover. **Diet:** Filters food particles from water. **Notes:** This mussel is popular as seafood, but may become poisonous after red tides.

Mytilus galloprovincialis
Family Mytilidae (Mussels)

Common
45 mm

Description: This shell is similar in shape and colour to *Choromytilus meridionalis* but smaller. The smooth exterior has radial growth-lines. **Colour:** Black or blue with a tinge of brown on lower surface and towards the umbo. **Habitat:** They form a dense band in the low intertidal zone. **Diet:** Filters food particles from water. **Notes:** This shell is a recent introduction from Europe and was rare at one time, but now it is the most abundant intertidal mussel on the Cape West coast. A fast-growing mussel that is cultivated for human consumption.

Perna perna
Family Mytilidae (Mussels)

Common
120 mm

Description: An elongate, wedge-shaped shell with a terminal umbo and a smooth surface. **Colour:** Purplish brown or yellowish brown. Periostracum is dark brown, yellowish brown to green. Interior is a shiny off-white with the colour of the exterior shining through. **Habitat:** The Brown Mussel is found in dense beds on rocky shores where water movement is brisk, both at the intertidal and infratidal zones down to about 5 m. **Diet:** Filters food particles from water. **Notes:** This species is the dominant mussel on the South and East coast of southern Africa.

Pinctada capensis
Family Pteriidae (Oysters)

Common
110 mm

Description: A relatively thick, heavy shell with a straight hinge-line. The right valve is shallower than the left valve. The byssal sinus is deep and wide. Sculpture of concentric wavy, coarse and densely packed lamellae. The wing-like projections on the valves are absent. **Colour:** Yellowish brown with darker brown radial bands. Nacreous interior has a grey border. **Habitat:** Mainly infratidal. Attached by byssus threads to rocks and reefs, also found in tidal pools. **Diet:** Filters food particles from water. **Notes:** This genus (not this species) is a source of pearls and mother-of-pearl.

Pinctada nigra
Family Pteriidae (Oysters)

Common
50 mm

Description: An ear-shaped, fragile, and often translucent shell. The valves are slightly uneven, and the byssal sinus is shallow. The early part of the shell is smooth but has growth-lines and flattened triangular lamellae towards the margin. **Colour:** Exterior is usually black with cream or off-white radiating rays, sometimes almost transparent. Interior is nacreous without a grey border, a grey fringe is present in juveniles. **Habitat:** Sheltered pools. **Diet:** Filters food particles from water. **Notes:** These molluscs may form extensive colonies in tidal swimming pools.

Atrina squamifera
Family Pinnidae (Pen Shells)

Uncommon
200 mm

Description: A wedge-shaped shell with rounded posterior margins at both ends. The exterior is sculptured by 8–12 radial ribs that bear spiny scales anteriorly. The internal surface has a thin nacreous layer that does not cover the entire posterior muscle scar. **Colour:** Brownish yellow. Umbonal area is darker. **Habitat:** Buried vertically with only the opening visible above the sand in lagoons, estuaries and protected bays. **Diet:** Filters food particles from water. **Notes:** The spiny scales of dense colonies can cause injury to bare feet.

Streptopinna saccata
Family Pinnidae (Pen Shells)

Uncommon
80 mm

Description: A thin, translucent and roughly orbicular shell. It appears markedly deformed with its thickened ventral margins, giving it an almost tube-like appearance. Sculptured by smooth, wide radial ribs, which are absent on the ventral slope. **Colour:** Pale cream, glossy brown to reddish brown. **Habitat:** Wedge-shaped crevices of submerged rocks or among marine growths such as the polyps of *Palythoa nelliae*. **Diet:** Filters food particles from water via gills. **Notes:** This animal usually settles in restricted areas between rocks, resulting in malformed, yet interesting, growth forms.

Lima lima vulgaris
Family Limidae (File Clams)

Uncommon
55 mm

Description: A semi-spherical shell, elongate towards the umbo. The exterior is sculptured by approximately 28 fairly coarse radiating ribs with strong scales. The anterior ear lacks the fine cross-striae found in *Lima nimbifer* (see p 124). The interior is glossy. The external ribs shine through. **Colour:** White, off-white. **Habitat:** Attached by byssus threads to rocks from low-tide level and deeper. **Diet:** Filters food particles from water. **Notes:** The single valves of this shell are quite common, but specimens with both valves intact are very rarely found.

Lima nimbifer
Family Limidae (File Clams)

Uncommon
40 mm

Description: An elongate, slightly oblique shell with compressed valves that gape slightly at each end. The ears are small. The anterior ear is weaker than the posterior ear, and is covered by fine transverse striae. Sculptured by 30–35 strong, rounded ribs, which bear erect scales. The ribs shine through. **Colour:** White. Interior is glossy and white. **Habitat:** Probably attached by byssus threads to rocks from low-tide level down to about 175 m. **Diet:** Filters food particles from water. **Notes:** Single valves wash up on beach but live animals are seldom seen.

Limaria tuberculata
Family Limidae (File Clams)

Uncommon
35 mm

Description: An oblique shell with inflated, spherical valves that gape at their anterior and posterior sides. The exterior is sculptured by thin radial ribs and is crossed by concentric growth-lines, rendering the surface weakly nodular. Fine radial threads occur on the ears and sides. **Colour:** White. **Habitat:** Usually found among large tunicates or in the holdfasts of kelp. Also lives under rocks at low-tide level down to about 40 m. **Diet:** Filters food particles from water. **Notes:** These animals are capable of swimming – they clap the valves together in order to achieve locomotion.

Crassostrea margaritacea
Family Ostreidae (Oysters)

Abundant
130 mm

Description: An elongate, heavy shell. The multi-layered lower valve is deep and cup-shaped, and is cemented to the substrate. Internally, the cavity is filled with progressive layers of shell. The upper valve has flat concentric lamellae with fine radial threads. **Colour:** Off-white with purplish-pink streaks. Lower valve has dark pink or purplish streaks. Interior tinged with purple. **Habitat:** Cape rock oysters form beds at extreme low tide, and further down. **Diet:** Filters food particles from water. **Notes:** This oyster is edible, and is the most dominant species south of the Transkei.

Saccostrea cuccullata
Family Ostreidae (Oysters)

Abundant
50 mm

Description: This shell is exceedingly variable in shape and outline. The lower valve has a deep recess under the hinge and is cemented to the rocks. The margins of the valves form undulating and interlocking folds that are normally tinged mauve. Upper valve flat with flat radial ribs mostly eroded. **Colour:** Valves are off-white, interior is glossy. **Habitat:** The Natal rock oyster forms a belt on rocks in the upper mid-tidal zone. Thrives in muddy conditions. **Diet:** Filters food particles from water. **Notes:** This edible species is the dominant oyster in KwaZulu-Natal.

Hyotissa numisma
Family Gryphaeidae

Rare
35 mm

Description: A small oyster with a thick, spherical shell and compressed valves. The exterior is rough while the interior is like porcelain. Under magnification the worn valves have a sponge-like appearance. **Colour:** Valves are uniform cream with radial rows of black or brown dots on the early part of the shell, which is particularly evident in juveniles. Sometimes with reddish or purple marks. **Habitat:** Under rocks in sheltered pools. **Diet:** Filters food particles from water via the gills. **Notes:** The black dots are a diagnostic feature.

Chlamys tincta
Family Pectinidae (Scallops)

Common
22 mm

Description: A small shell. The ventral margin is rounded and the valves, equal in shape and size, have a single ear. 50–70 fine radial ribs vary in thickness and bear small scales, which are prickly in fresh specimens and those from sheltered habitats. **Colour:** It comes in a variety of colours including orange, violet, reddish brown with cream flames and mottled brown. **Habitat:** Attached by byssus threads, amongst kelp holdfasts and large tunicates. **Diet:** Filters food particles from water. **Notes:** The commonest pecten in Southern Africa.

Pecten sulcicostatus

Family Pectinidae (Scallops)

Uncommon
80 mm

Description: A fairly large, orbicular shell with one inflated valve and one flat valve. The ears are of the same shape. The ribs on the inflated valve number between 12 and 15, and are wider than the intervals. The ribs on the flat valve are higher, flat topped and not wider than the intervals. **Colour:** Cream or buff with purple markings, flat valve is cream to pale pink throughout. Adult shells are paler, beach shells are pink. **Habitat:** Clean or muddy sand in water of 70–80 m. In shallower water in False Bay. **Diet:** Filters food particles from water. **Notes:** This scallop is able to swim by clapping the valves together.

Spondylus nicobaricus

Family Spondylidae (Thorny Oysters)

Common
35 mm

Description: An orbicular shell that may be oblique and elongate, deformed due to growth in rock crevices. The wings are equal in size. Sculptured by axial ridges bearing small erect, sharp spines. The bottom valve is attached to the rocks. **Colour:** White with red spots near umbo, the rest is dull red to scarlet. Early pattern of spotting may persist in adults. Interior is glossy white with a reddish-brown border. **Habitat:** Tidal swimming pools, intertidal zone. **Diet:** Filters food particles from water. **Notes:** Articulated shells are often found in tidal swimming pools.

Spondylus groschi
Family Spondylidae (Thorny Oysters)

Uncommon
75 mm

Description: This shell is similar to *S. nicobaricus* but larger, thicker and heavier. An orbicular shell with equal wings. Sculptured by radial ridges with upturned, almost spatula-shaped scales. Some ridges strong with weaker intermediate ones. **Colour:** Varies from orange-yellow to wine-red. Interior is porcelain-white with an orange or red border. **Habitat:** Rock crevices in lower intertidal zone and deeper. **Diet:** Filters food particles from water. **Notes:** The lower valve is always cemented to the substrate. Valves commonly wash up on the beach.

Divallinga dalliana
Family Lucinidae (Lucine Clams)

Common
28 mm

Description: This shell has an almost circular shape and inflated valves with a glossy surface. The shell is thin and has a central umbo. Curved ridges diverge along an axial line and form a smooth, off-centre ray in adults. Concentric growth lines may be present. The inner margin has fine teeth. **Colour:** White to flesh. **Habitat:** Clean sand below low-tide level, down to 25 m. Complete shells are rarely found in beach drift. **Diet:** Filters food particles from water. **Notes:** This animal creates a mucus-lined tube in the sand, which it uses in order to filter food particles from the water.

Chama lazarus
Family Chamidae (Jewel Boxes)

Uncommon
50 mm

Description: An oval or roughly orbicular, inflated shell. The surface is composed of strong, concentric, upturned leaf-like lamellae arranged from umbo to margin. The inner margin is smooth. **Colour:** Variable, often white throughout. Also lemon and yellow or red at the umbo, has one or two reddish-brown radial rays. The inside is white. **Habitat:** Extreme low-tide level, and deeper. **Diet:** Filters food particles from water. **Notes:** Only juveniles wash up on the beach. The lower valve is always cemented to rocks or coral.

Chama limbula
Family Chamidae (Jewel Boxes)

Common
60 mm

Description: A somewhat elongate, heavy shell that is usually eroded. The umbo of the lower or left valve is strongly curved to the right. The exterior of the upper valve has concentric upturned lamellae on the scales. The posterior third is separated by a shallow, wide groove. **Colour:** Exterior is chalky, usually encrusted with marine growth. Interior is porcelain-white with purple margins. **Habitat:** Shallow pools, sometimes in small colonies. **Diet:** Filters food particles from water. **Notes:** Lower valve is cemented to rock or coral.

Cardita variegata
Family Carditidae (Cardita Clams)

Common
34 mm

Description: An elongate, oblique and heavy shell, inflated with terminal umbones and indented midway on the ventral margin. Sculptured by 20–25 coarse, rounded radial ribs. Wider posteriorly and across the middle. A densely ornamented surface with blunt scales or nodules. **Colour:** Exterior is cream or buff, ridges are spotted and blotched with reddish brown. Interior is porcelain-white with external spots shining through. **Habitat:** Attached to underside of rocks in low-tide pools. **Diet:** Filters food particles from water. **Notes:** Animal attaches itself with byssus threads.

Thecalia concamerata
Family Carditidae (Cardita Clams)

Common
18 mm

Description: This shell is similar to *C. variegata* but smaller. A shell with a folded ventral margin that forms a deep brood-pouch on the inside of each valve in which the young are incubated. The pouch is only present in individuals larger than 10 mm. Sculptured by 14–20 coarse radial ribs with upturned scales. **Colour:** Cream on ridges with a dirty-brown, thin and smooth periostracum in the interspaces. Interior is glossy white. **Habitat:** Attached to underside of rocks in low-tide pools. **Diet:** Filters food particles from water. **Notes:** These clams are known as 'Ghost Hands' in Jeffreys Bay.

Eucrassatella sowerbyi
Family Crassatellidae (Crassatellas)

Common
24 mm

Description: An elongate, trigonal shell. The umbo occurs near the anterior end. The tapering posterior end is longer than the anterior end. The exterior is sculptured by coarse growth-lines. **Colour:** Valves are buff to brownish yellow with radial streaks, oblique wavy brown lines, or rows of brown dots. The smooth, thin yellowish-brown periostracum is firmly attached to the shell. White interior is tinged with pink towards the umbo. **Habitat:** Offshore on sandy bottoms. Single valves often wash up. **Diet:** Filters food particles from water. **Notes:** Two colour forms occur – one with brown lines; the other is uniformly brown.

Trachycardium rubicundum
Family Cardiidae (Cockles)

Common
50 mm

Description: An oval, inflated, thick shell with a centrally placed umbo. Sculptured by 36 flattened radial ribs with triangular scales facing upwards. The ribs protrude at the margin, forming sharp serrations with marked intervals. **Colour:** Beige to light brown, mottled with brown and purplish pink. Interior is white with a bright red margin and hinge-line. **Habitat:** Single valves commonly wash up on the beach but live shells live below the tide-line in sand pockets. **Diet:** Uses siphon to filter food particles from water. **Notes:** Red margin on the valves is a diagnostic feature.

Tridacna squamosa
Family Tridacnidae (Giant Clams)

Uncommon
220 mm

Description: An elongate, almost equilateral shell with a wide gape at the umbo through which the byssus threads protrude. Sculptured by 4–12 rounded ribs expanding rapidly in width from umbo to margin. The ribs bear scales that become progressively bigger towards the margin. The aperture is curved. The colourful mantle projects through the aperture. **Colour:** White, tinged with orange. **Diet:** Filter feeder. **Habitat:** Shallow water, attached to rocks. **Notes:** This animal houses algae in its tissues to produce food through photosynthesis.

Lutraria lutraria
Family Mactridae (Trough Shells)

Common
90 mm

Description: A large, elongate and thin shell that gapes at both ends. The exterior is fairly smooth and sculptured by concentric growth-lines. **Colour:** White with brownish stains. The periostracum is greyish brown, the interior is white. **Habitat:** Immobile in lagoons and infratidally, deeply buried (about 30 cm) in clean or muddy sand. **Diet:** The long non-retractable siphon breaks the sand surface to draw in food particles. **Notes:** Live shells frequently wash up on the beach where they are eaten by seagulls.

Mactra glabrata
Family Mactridae (Trough Shells)

Common
90 mm

Description: A fairly large, trigonal and inflated shell with distinctly gaping ends. Sculptured by thin concentric threads at the anterior and the posterior margin of the valve. **Colour:** Cream with faint radial lines in juveniles. **Habitat:** Generally infratidal. Burrows just below surface in fine sand in sheltered low-tide banks. **Diet:** Deposit feeder, collects food through siphon from surface of sand. **Notes:** The Atlantic form is replaced eastward by a smaller Indian Ocean form known as *M. g. lilacea*, which has strong concentric threads on the anterior half of shell.

Scissodesma spengleri
Family Mactridae (Trough Shells)

Common
92 mm

Description: A large, trigonal shell with centrally placed, widely separated umbones. The valves are almost equilateral with the posterior margin formed into a broad flattened surface with a sharp ridge radiating from the umbo. The shell is smooth with radiating striae. **Colour:** White with a thin brown periostracum. Interior is white. **Habitat:** Burrows shallowly in clean sand from the low-tide level down to 8 m. **Diet:** Deposit feeder that collects food through a long siphon. **Notes:** Double shells wash up in large numbers after storms.

Solen capensis
Family Solenidae (Razor Shells)

Common
85 mm

Description: A narrow and elongate shell, parallel-sided but almost cylindrical in cross section with widely gaping ends. The anterior end is oblique and the edge is bent outwards, demarcated by a groove. Sculpture of growth-lines only. **Colour:** Valves are off-white, tinged with pale pinkish brown. Interior is white; sometimes tinged with violet. Periostracum is thin, tinged with green. **Habitat:** Lagoons and estuaries, burrows into clean sand at low-tide level down to about 1 m. **Diet:** Suspension feeders. **Notes:** These animals are known as 'Pencilbait', and are used as bait by fishermen.

Solen cylindraceus
Family Solenidae (Razor Shells)

Common
75 mm

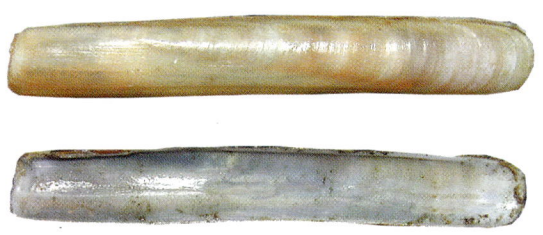

Description: Similar to *S. capensis* but smaller and narrower; lacks groove demarcating lip at the anterior end. The outer surface is fairly smooth with concentric growth-lines. **Colour:** Periostracum is greenish brown to pinkish brown. Shell is usually brown, often tinged with pink. **Habitat:** Estuaries in soft mud banks just above the low spring-tide level. **Diet:** Filters suspended food particles through a short siphon. **Notes:** This species replaces *S. capensis* in KwaZulu-Natal where anglers know it as 'Stickbait'. The two species occur together in estuaries of the Eastern Cape.

Gastrana matadoa

Family Tellinidae (Tellins)

Common

30 mm

Description: An oval and swollen shell. The posterior end is angular and the umbo is situated towards the anterior side. Sculptured by fine concentric growth-lines, which are crossed by fine radial striae. The shell is sometimes distorted. **Colour:** White and often tinged with orange towards the umbo. **Habitat:** Infratidal. In estuaries and sheltered sandbanks. **Diet:** Siphon projects from sand, used for searching for food deposited on sand. **Notes:** Shells with both valves intact frequently wash up on the beach. Known as 'Handbags' in Jeffreys Bay.

Tellina alfredensis

Family Tellinidae (Tellins)

Common

65 mm

Description: An oval, elongate shell with a tapering posterior end. The valves are laterally compressed and bent slightly to the right. The left valve is deeper than the right. Sculpture of weak radial grooves and very fine concentric threads that become coarser at both ends. **Colour:** Valves are pink, more vivid on inside. **Habitat:** Below the tide levels down to about 3 m. **Diet:** Burrows in clean sand using the long siphon to suck in particles from the surface. **Notes:** The vivid colours of live shells fade quickly after exposure to air and light.

Tellina gilchristi
Family Tellinidae (Tellins)

Uncommon
25 mm

Description: An elongate shell. The posterior end is tapering, while the anterior end is rounded. Sculpture of fine, weak concentric threads. **Colour:** Valves are white or pink with concentric bands of darker pink with pinkish-white axial rays, sometimes uniform white. Umbo is occasionally tinged with a salmon colour. **Habitat:** Infratidally down to 100 m. May occur in sheltered bays at low-tide level. Burrows in clean sand. **Diet:** Long siphon is used to collect food particles deposited on the sand. **Notes:** The pink rays distinguish it from other small Cape species.

Tellina trilatera
Family Tellinidae (Tellins)

Common
45 mm

Description: A triangular, thin shell. The anterior end is broadly rounded while the tapering posterior end is elongate and not flexed. The umbo is situated towards the anterior end. Sculpture of very fine concentric striae, but may have prominent growth-lines. **Colour:** Exterior is white and glossy with a thin, pale brown and glossy periostracum. Interior is glossy white. **Habitat:** Burrows in fine sand infratidally down to about 8 m. **Diet:** Uses siphon to feed on particles from sand surface. **Notes:** A common species, particularly in False Bay and the Western Cape.

Donax serra

Family Donacidae (Donax Clams)

Common
65 mm

Description: A heavy, oval to trigonal shell with a short, tapering posterior end. Sculptured by weak, shallow radial striae that become deeper posteriorly. The postero-dorsal region bears wavy concentric ridges. The inner margin has weak teeth. **Colour:** Exterior of the valves is white, yellow or pale purple. Periostracum is olive-brown. Interior is violet or salmon-pink. **Habitat:** Intertidal region, burrows in sand. **Diet:** Deposit feeder that sucks in food particles through siphon. **Notes:** These animals are popular as bait, and are known as white mussels.

Trapezium bicarinatum

Family Trapeziidae (Trapezium Clams)

Uncommon
50 mm

Description: A thick, moderately inflated shell that is shaped like a trapeze. The posterior end is elongate with a strong umbonal ridge. Sculptured by coarse concentric growth-lines, which are crossed by radial striae giving the shell a nodular appearance. **Colour:** Periostracum is pale yellowish brown. External and internal colour is white, sometimes with a purple hinge. **Habitat:** Lower intertidal zone, nestling in crevices in rocks and coral boulders, attached to substratum by byssus threads. **Diet:** Filters food particles from water. **Notes:** This species also occurs in Australia.

Trapezium sowerbyi
Family Trapeziidae (Trapezium Clams)

Uncommon
100 mm

Description: This shell is similar to *T. bicarinatum* but bigger, heavier and markedly inflated. The exterior is sculptured by prominent concentric growth-lines and radial ridges, rendering the surface nodular, which is more conspicuous towards the margin. **Colour:** White with a yellowish-brown or pink postero-dorsal region, and with wine-red radial lines or streaks. Interior is white. **Habitat:** Anchored by byssus threads to crevices in infratidal rocks and coral. **Diet:** Filters food particles from water. **Notes:** Single valves commonly wash up on the beach but articulated specimens are rare.

Tivela compressa
Family Veneridae (Venus Clams)

Uncommon
55 mm

Description: A thick, trigonal and somewhat inflated shell with a rounded ventral margin. The umbo is high and central. The smooth and glossy outer surface has fine concentric growth-lines. **Colour:** Exterior is pale brown with darker radiating rays and wavy, dull reddish-brown concentric lines. Interior is white. **Habitat:** Infratidal region, in 2–50 m, burrows in clean sand where only the siphon protrudes above the sand. **Diet:** Food particles are drawn in by the siphon. **Notes:** These bivalves frequently wash up in large numbers in False Bay after storms.

Tivela polita
Family Veneridae (Venus Clams)

Common
40 mm

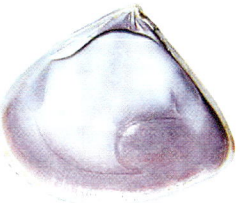

Description: This shell is smaller than *T. compressa*, and is trigonal and compressed. The anterior end is rounded, while the posterior end is angular. The dorsal margin is straight and the central umbo has a pointed apex. The outer surface is glossy and smooth with weak growth-lines. **Colour:** Exterior is yellowish brown with darker and lighter reddish-brown rays. Interior is white and tinged with violet. The glossy periostracum is thin and firmly attached to the shell. **Habitat:** Burrows in fine sand below tide-level. **Diet:** Feeds on food particles deposited on the sand. **Notes:** Also known as sand mussels; used as bait by fishermen.

Tivela platyaulax
Family Veneridae (Venus Clams)

Uncommon
32 mm

Description: An obliquely trigonal, thick and heavy shell. The umbo is situated towards the anterior end and curves inwards. Sculptured by approximately eight strong concentric ridges. The interstices are V-shaped. **Colour:** Exterior is cream to yellowish white, speckled with reddish brown, and covered with two to three interrupted reddish-brown radiating rays. Interior is white, sometimes tinged with violet. **Habitat:** Infratidal, in sand. **Diet:** Deposited food particles are collected by siphon. **Notes:** Single valves commonly wash up on the beach, but complete specimens are rare.

Gafrarium pectinatum alfredense
Family Veneridae (Venus Clams)

Common
20 mm

Description: An oval, inflated shell. The posterior end is less rounded than the anterior end. Sculptured by well-developed rounded radial ribs, which tend to split towards the margin. Some curved ribs diverge from the radial ribs towards the dorsal margin.
Colour: Variable: pale to dirty cream to light orange, speckled and blotched with brown or reddish brown. **Habitat:** Sand in rock pools at the infratidal fringe. Single shells commonly wash up on beach.
Diet: Food particles are gathered from sand. **Notes:** Colour variation may cause confusion with identification.

Gafrarium divaricatum
Family Veneridae (Venus Clams)

Uncommon
32 mm

Description: This shell is similar to *G. pectinatum alfredense* but bigger and less inflated. The shell is oval, thick and tapers posteriorly. Sculptured by radiating ribs, which diverge towards the margin. The ribs are crossed by concentric growth-lines. The inner margin has weak teeth. **Colour:** White, flecked with purplish brown, interior tinged with violet-brown. **Habitat:** Sheltered bays in muddy sand, between rocks at the low-tide fringe and in deeper water. **Diet:** Collects food particles with a siphon. **Notes:** Articulated specimens can sometimes be collected on the beach.

Venerupis corrugata
Family Veneridae (Venus Clams)

Common
45 mm

Description: A shell that is variable in shape, colour and sculpture. Oval and thick, with an anterior umbo. Sculptured by wavy concentric threads in the posterodorsal region. The surface may appear rough. **Colour:** Cream, buff, light brown, either uniform or with a pattern of radial blotches, flames, brownish streaks or specks, tinged pink towards umbo. **Habitat:** In sand from low-tide level down to 25 m. **Diet:** Food particles are collected by the siphon. **Notes:** Shells are big and drab in colder water and small, more vivid in the warmer water of False Bay.

Venus verrucosa
Family Veneridae (Venus Clams)

Common
40 mm

Description: An oval to spherical, very heavy shell. The hooked umbones are situated anteriorly. Sculpture of strong concentric ridges, which break up into rounded nodules near the margin. Radial grooves diverge anteriorly and posteriorly. **Colour:** Base colour is cream with brown radial rays, sometimes tinged with pink or with faint zigzag purplish lines. **Habitat:** Burrows in clean sand or gravel, with posterior end exposed, from low-tide level down to 155 m. **Diet:** Filters particles from the sand. **Notes:** The exposed posterior end is frequently coloured green by algae.

FURTHER READING

Barnard, K.H. 1953. *A Beginners Guide to South African Shells*. Maskew Miller Limited, Cape Town.

Branch, G.M., Griffiths, C.L., Branch, M.L. & Beckley, L.E. 1994. *Two Oceans: A Guide to the Marine Life of Southern Africa*. David Philip, Cape Town & Johannesburg.

Kilburn, R. & Rippey, E. 1982. *Sea Shells of Southern Africa*. Macmillan, Johannesburg.

Kensley, B. 1973. *Sea Shells of Southern Africa: Gastropods*. Maskew Miller Limited, Cape Town.

Richards, D. 1984. *South African Shells: A Collector's Guide*. C. Struik (Pty) Ltd, Cape Town.

Steyn, D.G. & Lussi, M. 1998. *Marine Shells of South Africa*. Ekogilde Publishers, Hartebeespoort.

Steyn, D.G. & Steyn, E.J. 1999. *The Sea Shells of Jeffreys Bay*. Eldolise Publishers, Pretoria.

SCIENTIFIC INDEX

Achanthochitona
  garnoti 114
Afrocominella
  elongata 73
Akera soluta 108
Amalda
  contusa 87
  obtusa 88
Arca avellana 118
Architectonica
  gualtierii 59
  perspectiva 60
Argobuccinum
  pustulosum 57
Argonauta argo 115
Atrina squamifera 122
Aulacomya ater 119
Babylonia
  papillaris 77
Barbatia
  foliata 118
  obliquata 119
Bufoneria crumena 52
Bulla ampulla 107
Bullia
  annulata 77
  callosa 78
  digitalis 79
  diluta 79
  laevissima 78
  mozambicensis 81
  natalensis 80
  pura 80
Burnupena
  catarrhacta 76
  cincta 74

  lagenaria 74
  limbosa 75
  papyracea 76
  pubescens 75
Bursa
  bufonia 52
  granularis 51
  rosa 51
Cabestana cutacea 54
Calliostoma
  ornatum 20
Callipara
  bullatiana 91
Callochiton
  dentatus 110
Calyptraea
  chinensis 32
Cardita
  variegata 130
Chaetopleura
  papilio 111
  pertusa 111
Chama
  lazarus 129
  limbula 129
Charonia lampas
  pustulata 53
Chicoreus
  austramosus 62
  ramosus 62
Chiton tulipa 113
Chlamys tincta 126
Choromytilus
  meridionalis 120
Clanculus
  puniceus 20

Clionella
  bornii 98
  krausii 99
  rosaria 100
  sinuata 98
  tripartita 99
Colubraria obscura 87
Conus
  betulinus 100
  biliosus 101
  catus 101
  chaldeus 102
  ebraeus 102
  flavidus 103
  lividus 103
  miles 104
  natalis 104
  rattus 105
  tinianus 105
Coralliophila
  fritschi 71
  squamosissima 72
Crassostrea
  margaritacea 125
Crepidula
  porcellana 33
Cronia
  margariticola 66
  ochrostoma 65
Cymatium
  aquatile 55
  closeli 56
  parthenopium 54
  pileare 55
Cymbula
  compressa 16

granatina 17
miniata 15
oculus 16
Cypraea
  annulus 43
  arabica immanis 45
  capensis 41
  caputserpentis 45
  chinensis 42
  citrina 41
  edentula 40
  erosa 44
  fuscodentata 40
  helvola 44
  histrio 46
  moneta 43
  tigris 46
  vitellus 42
Cypraecassis rufa 49
Demoulia
  abbreviata 82
  ventricosa 81
Dendrofissurella
  scutellum 13
Dentalium
  regulare 116
Diloma
  sinensis 22
  tabularis 23
  tigrina 21
  variegata 22
Dinoplax
  fossus 112
  gigas 112
  validifossus 113
Diodora
  calyculata 14
  elizabethae 14
Distorsio anus 58
Divallinga dalliana 128
Donax serra 137
Drupa
  morum 64
  ricinus 64
Eucrassatella
  sowerbyi 131
Fasciolaria
  lugubris 84
  heynemanni 85
Ficus ficus 50
Fusinus ocelliferus 84
Gafrarium
  divaricatum 140
  pectinatum
    alfredense 140
Gastrana matadoa 135

Glycymeris
  connollyi 117
  queketti 117
Gyrineum pusillum 57
Gyroscala
  coronata 58
  lamellosa 59
Haliotis
  midae 12
  parva 13
  spadicea 12
Harpa
  amouretta 91
  major 92
Helcion concolor 19
Hydatina
  amplustre 106
  physis 106
  zonata 107
Hyotissa
  numisma 126
Janthina
  janthina 60
  prolongata 61
Lambis
  lambis 31
  truncata 32
Lamellaria nigra 36
Latirus
  abnormis 86
  turritus 86
Lima
  lima vulgaris 123
  nimbifer 124
Limaria
  tuberculata 124
Lutraria lutraria 132
Mactra glabrata 133
Mancinella
  alouina 66
  echinulata 67
Marginella
  lussii 94
  mosaica 93
  ornata 92
  rosea 93
Melapium lineatum 90
Mipus rosaceus 72
Mitra
  latruncularia 95
  limbifera 95
  litterata 96
  picta 94
  punctostriata 96
Monodonta australis 21
Morula granulata 65

Murex brevispina 61
Mytilus
  galloprovincialis 120
Nassa francolina 70
Nassarius
  glans fenwicki 83
  speciosus 82
Natica
  allapapilionis 33
  tecta 34
Nerita
  albicilla 26
  polita 27
  textiles 27
  undata 28
Neverita
  didyma 35
  peselephanti 34
Nodilittorina
  africana 29
  knysnaensis 28
Nucella
  cingulata 69
  dubia 69
  squamosa 70
Oliva
  bulbosa 89
  caroliniana 88
  tigrina 89
  tremulina 90
Onithochiton
  literatus 114
Pecten
  sulcicostasus 127
Peristernia
  forskalii 85
Perna perna 121
Phalium
  areola 48
  fimbria 48
Phenacovolva
  aurantia 39
  brevirostris 38
  rosea 38
Pinctada
  capensis 121
  nigra 122
Polinices mamilla 35
Pteropurpura
  graagae 63
  uncinaria 63
Pupillaea aperta 15
Purpura panama 67
Ranella australasia
  gemmifera 56
Rapana rapiformis 71

Saccostrea
   cuccullata 125
Scissodesma
   spengleri 133
Scutellastra
   argenvillei 17
   cochlear 18
   longicosta 18
   tabularis 19
Semicassis labiata
   iredalei 47
Semicassis labiata
   zeylanica 47
Sepia officinalis
   vermiculata 116
Siphonaria
   capensis 109
   concinna 110
   oculus 109
Solen
   capensis 134
   cylindraceus 134
Spirula spirula 115
Spondylus
   groschi 128
   nicobaricus 127

Streptopinna
   saccata 123
Strombus decorus 30
   gibberulus 31
   mutabilis 30
Tellina
   alfredensis 135
   gilchristi 136
   trilatera 136
Thais
   bufo 68
   capensis 68
Thecalia
   concamerata 130
Tivela
   compressa 138
   platyaulax 139
   polita 139
Tonna
   perdix 50
   variegata 49
Trachycardium
   rubicundum 131
Trapezium
   bicarinatum 137
   sowerbyi 138

Tricolia capensis 26
Tridacna squamosa 132
Trigonostoma
   foveolata 97
   semidisjuncta 97
Trivia
   aperta 36
   magnidentata 37
   ovulata 37
Trochus
   nigropunctatus 23
Turbo
   cidaris 25
   coronatus 24
   miliaris 25
   sarmaticus 24
Turitella carinifera 29
Tutufa bubo 53
Umbraculum
   umbraculum 118
Vasum truncatum 83
Venerupis
   corrugata 141
Venus verrucosa 143
Volema pyrum 73
Volva kilburni 99